Plants for Connoisseurs

HOUSE & GARDEN BOOK OF

Plants for Connoisseurs

chosen by Peter Coats

COLLINS—LONDON & GLASGOW IN ASSOCIATION WITH
THE CONDÉ NAST PULICIATIONS LTD

Published by COLLINS—LONDON & GLASGOW
in association with THE CONDÉ NAST PUBLICATIONS LTD
COPYRIGHT © 1974 THE CONDÉ NAST PUBLICATIONS LTD
ISBN 0 00 435071 5

Contents

The photographs in this book were taken by the author, with the exception of a few pictures contributed by George Archer, Gerard Bellot, Boucher, Brodrick Haldane, Horst, Lamontagne, Georges Leveque, Lyon, Patrick Matthews, Tania Midgley, C. Readjones, T. H. Reimer, Valerie Roach, Henri Rousselle, Michael Wickham

Introduction

The object of this book is to list the very best varieties of the most popular plant families. For instance, of the hundreds of viburnums in cultivation, and of the thousands of roses, I have indicated the comparatively few which from my own experience - and the experience of experts - are the best viburnum and roses to choose. It is a book for gardeners who want to grow in their gardens, the best plants, and what is just as important, the best plants that are available.

It would be pointless to urge gardeners to grow Eritrichium nanum which Reginald Farrer once extolled in his purplest passage but which the RHS dictionary dismisses as "not a success in cultivation"; or to expatiate on the charms of that little known climber Wattakaka sinensis. Both plants are seldom listed in catalogues and hardly repay the trouble they take to grow.

It is important, in any illustrated book on plants, for the plants to be shown in scale. There are magnificent plant dictionaries - which are far more comprehensive than *Plants for Connoisseurs* - in which potentilla flowers are shown as large as peonies, and clematis as small as daisies. In choosing the illustrations for this book I have endeavoured, whenever I can, to show the plants in scale.

My friend, the late Victoria Sackville-West whose word was gospel to the thousands of readers who read her articles every week, once wrote that, when asked what her aim would be if required to plant a garden where space was restricted, her answer was, to choose only the very best varieties in every group. It was the soundest possible advice, and what one would expect from a very great gardener. I dedicate this book, with affection, to her memory.

PETER COATS
Al Albany, W1

7

Architectural form

Plants have been the inspiration of architects for centuries. The Greeks used the leaves of the acanthus as a model for the capitals of their Corinthian columns. And the honeysuckle inspired the anthemion, a motif which recurs constantly in the decorative schemes of the Ancients. In the eighteenth century the tassels of Garrya elliptica are said to have given the Adam brothers the idea for the slender garlands which are a feature of many of their designs; though this can hardly be so, as garrya was only introduced into Europe from Oregon in 1828, when both James and Robert Adam were dead. But as many of the Adams' designs were inspired by the Etruscans, who used swags of leaves and catkins to make a similar effect, perhaps that is how the garrya story originated.

Plants of architectural form give body and importance to any planting scheme: their leaves, even when deciduous, are often long lasting, and their shapes and textures are so different that, with the plants we have at our command today, it is possible to create a border composed only of architectural plants, which can be extremely effective.

Though deciduous plants, as they die down in winter, are, perhaps, a degree less useful in a garden than evergreens, when they are in full foliage they can be magnificent. Acanthus, already mentioned, is one of the very best; so much so that that great gardener, Victoria Sackville-West praised the prickly Acanthus spinosissimus as, "very showy in July" and went on to say, with typical humour - "For some odd reason, it is popularly known as Bear's Breeches, though I should be very sorry for any bear that

Opposite *All the yuccas are plants of handsome architectural bearing, with superb heads of white bell-shaped flowers and swordlike leaves. Y. gloriosa has the* *stiffest, sharpest leaves; Y. filamentosa, foliage that is edged with thready hairs*
Above *Prunus serrulata erecta Amanogawa makes a soaring pillar of white* *blossom. Its Japanese name, Amanogawa means "Milky-way". It is a flowering cherry which associates especially well with architecture*

9

Campanula persicifolia alba, one of the most handsome of Bell Flowers, echoes the sculptured shapes of closely clipped yew trees

had to wear them."

Angelica is another plant of fine sculptured form, especially when its boldly chiselled leaves are surmounted by its green globes of seed-heads. Alliums - especially the roundheaded sphaerocephalum, make very effective architectural interjections, as do the towering, grey leaved bocconias, and there are many others.

But it is the evergreen, or ever-grey, plants of well defined form, which are of the greatest value in the garden.

Few plants offer as noble an outline as the yucca - a most exotic looking Mexican member of the lily family, which good humouredly condescends to thrive in Northern gardens. Vibur-

num cylindricum, that waxy-leaved Wayfaring Tree which has made its way to Western gardens from the Himalayas and won affection for its heart-warming gift of glinting foliage for all the gardening year, is another; and the mahonias, especially the handsome lomariifolia, magnolias such as grandiflora, and the slender light hearted brooms (especially if trimmed each year after flowering) are all plants which can give form and shape to the garden all the year round. When there are no flowers, they make the framework of the garden, and bring the valued gift of colour. They are real friends in need - and in a less formal, and more interesting way, they fulfil the function which topiary did in the larger gardens of the past.

Leaf contrast in a well planted border – in the foreground, grey cushions of Santolina Chamaecyparissus. Behind, the towering golden flowered spires of Verbascum Chaixii, with the silver mauve flower heads of Salvia turkestanica beyond

Acanthus (*Acanthaceae*) Acanthus mollis and A. spinosissimus are two of the finest foliage plants for the shrub border, or in half shade. Their magnificent leaves were the inspiration of classical architects.

Achillea (*Compositae*) The achilleas all have finely modelled flower heads which give form and shape to any planting scheme. The best of the yarrows are the ever popular Gold Plate (excellent for drying), Moonshine, a pleasing pale yellow with silvery leaves, and A. ptarmica "The Pearl", white and useful for cutting.

Aegle (*Rutaceae*) Aegle sepiaria in a sheltered position, will bear small orange-like fruit on its green spiny branches. Its flowers are white.

Agapanthus (*Liliaceae*) One of the most distinguished of all tub-plants, the African Lily bears its umbels of blue flowers in July. The Headbourne Hybrids are the hardiest, and will thrive in the open ground.

Allium (*Liliaceae*) The ornamental onions can bring unique forms and some subtle colouring to the herbaceous border in late summer. A. Beesianum has pale blue flowers, flavum, hanging bells of yellow, macranthum, mauve bells in July, A. karataviense has handsome, variegated leaves, and A. nobile is the

Above *Two plants of architectural form in one picture. To the left, Acanthus mollis, the leaves of which were the models for the Greeks when designing their Corinthian capitals – and to the right, and in sharp contrast, the imposing foliage of the New Zealand Flax, Phormium tenax*
Below *Eucomis bicolor, a bulbous plant of good outline, with columns of greenish star-shaped flowers and luxuriant leaves. It flowers in late summer, and needs wall-shelter in cold climates*
Opposite *Eremurus Bungei, the noble Foxtail Lily, flowers in early summer – it appreciates sharp drainage, and a place in the sun. The recently raised Highdown Hybrids, which flower in alluring tints of coral, amber and different golds, are an improvement on the form*

tallest and largest flowered.

Angelica (*Umbelliferae*) For fine architectural form there are few plants more rewarding than Archangelica officinalis, with its almost spherical heads of flowers and seeds. It usually dies after flowering, but generously seeds itself about. It does best in a moist situation and half shade.

Bocconia (*Papaveraceae*) This handsome relation of the poppies, in its best form, B. cordata (syn. Macleaya cordata) looks well, planted under trees or in a shrubbery. It will thrive in any rich, light soil, but likes plenty of room.

Cortaderia (*Gramineae*) Several of the Pampas Grasses can provide handsome outlines for the garden in late summer. Cortaderia argentea is the usual silver headed form. C. carnea has plumes tinted with pink, while C. compacta is a miniature Pampas Grass which could find a place in the smallest garden.

Crambe (*Cruciferae*) This is one of the great border and shrubbery plants – making four foot high rosettes of vast cabbage leaves, surmounted by a cloud of white flowers in July. The variety Kotschyana is said to have particularly large flowers (RHS Dictionary).

Cynara (*Compositae*) The artichokes, with their sculptured silver leaves, can contribute magnificent form to the mixed border. The Cardoon, C. Cardunculus is the most imposing.

Datura (*Solanaceae*) Daturas, in tubs

Above *The soaring outline of Heracleum Mantegazzianum, the Giant Hemlock, or cow-parsley, in a garden which might be in Kyoto, but is actually in Berkshire. Though magnificent to look at, the heracleums are prolific seeders, and best relegated to the wilder parts of the garden, and away from small gardens altogether*

Below *Few plants have handsomer leaves than the Giant Cardoon – Cynara Cardunculus*

Opposite *A border at Pyrford Court in Surrey in which the cool glaucous tones of columnar cypresses, such as Cupressus glabra pyramidalis, echo the grey-green foliage of dianthus and senecio*

Above *Bursting like fireworks, the spectacular leaves of two dracaenas, palm-like plants which are hardier than they seem, and below a close plantation of Berberis buxifolia from the Magellan straits, with Bergenia cordifolia and acanthus*

Opposite *Three pictures in each of which is shown one of the best of all the shrubby spurges, Euphorbia Wulfenii. Above it appears in juxtaposition with Yucca gloriosa, below and to the left as companion to a graceful statue, and to the right as neighbour to one of the best of ceanothus, C. thyrsiflorus. Euphorbia Wulfenii shows its huge heads of acid green flower in early spring, and is a plant of the greatest pictorial value*

or boxes, lend an exotic and very special air to any terrace, but have to be wintered in the greenhouse. D. suaveolens, The Angel's Trumpet is the most beautiful white, scented datura. D. sanguinea has orange flowers.

Dicentra (*Papaveraceae*) The Bleeding Heart, D. spectabilis, has deeply cut glaucous leaves and attractive, elegantly arching stems of curiously shaped rosy pink flowers. It should be given a position which is sheltered from spring frosts. Valuable for its unique habit.

Dracaena (*Liliaceae*) Dracaenas will grow well in protected gardens in the south and strike an exotic note in any border in which they are planted. D.

Draco is the Dragon Tree, one of the longest lived plants in nature, and a native of the Canary Islands.

Eremurus (*Liliaceae*) Eremurus or Fox Tail Lilies, are among the noblest of the lily family, and make spires of pale flowers – in white, cream or yellow in summer. E. Bungei is one of the most imposing. Highdown Gold has particularly lucent flowers.

Eryngium (*Umbelliferae*) The Sea Hollies have decorative blue-green foliage and flower heads encircled by spiny bracts. The most beautiful to grow are alpinum, with incredibly delicate ruffs of foliage – pandanifolium, with fine exotic leaves but nondescript flowers,

and the purple amethystinum. Eryngiums like light soil and full sun, and do well by the sea.

Eucomis (*Liliaceae*) At the base of a warm, south facing wall, in well drained soil is where E. comosa is most likely to succeed. Its exotic flowers are greenish white and borne on columnar stems which can reach a foot or more in length. But it is a plant only for favoured climates.

Euphorbia (*Euphorbiaceae*) These are some of the most popular connoisseur's plants of today, and few gardens can be considered complete without at least one euphorbia. Varieties to look for, are the herbaceous E. griffithii with orange red bracts, and E. polychroma with brilliant acid-green flowers in early spring. Good shrubby euphorbias include the splendid E. Wulfenii, the best of all, the quick spreading dark green leaved E. robbiae and the trailing jade-leaved E. Myrsinites. E. pulcherrima is the popular greenhouse plant poinsettia.

Foeniculum (*Umbelliferae*) Fennel makes a three-foot high feathery plant, equally useful for its graceful form, and its value in cooking. The Bronze Fennel is particularly attractive – but can seed itself about rather too freely.

Garrya (*Garryaceae*) The male form of Garrya elliptica presents a splendid appearance in winter when its branches are hung with its characteristic long glaucous catkins. Garrya thrives by the seaside, but is tolerant of town conditions.

Above *In a setting of different grasses (Festuca glauca to the right) Hyacinthus candicans raises its bell towers of pure white flowers. Also known as galtonias, hyacinthus brings welcome fresh colouring to the garden in early autumn*

Below *In contrast to the cool flowers of Hyacinthus candicans, kniphofia shows altogether warmer tints; Red Hot Pokers flower in late summer and K. uvaria, H. C. Mills, shown here, is one of the most prolific*

Opposite *Pampas Grass, Cortaderia argentea, holds its handsome heads up in the second half of summer. These persist in beauty until the first frosts*

Its swags are said to have inspired the Adam brothers.

Heracleum (*Umbelliferae*) The Giant Cow Parsleys present a superb architectural outline, but should only be grown in the wilder parts of the garden, as they are prolific seeders and can become a nuisance. Their huge forked leaves are most impressive, and their soaring stems terminating in vast umbels of cream coloured flowers are magnificent. For bigger, better leaves – and

fewer unwanted seedlings – the flower heads should be cut down as soon as they start to fade. Heracleum Mantegazzianum is the one to look for.

Lavatera (*Malvaceae*) The Tree Mallows, especially Lavatera Olbia with its many rose-coloured flowers and downy, hand-shaped leaves, make handsome shrubs, and will thrive on chalk and by the sea. L. maritima has bold white flowers. Of the annual mallows, Pink Domino and White Lady are outstanding.

Morina (*Dipsaceae*) Morina has singular leaves which are spined like a thistle and long spikes of white and crimson flowers in whorls. It is an excellent subject for the front of a shrub border, and will thrive in any well drained soil. M. longifolia is the best.

Myosotidium (*Boraginaceae*) This is a real connoisseur's plant, but not of the easiest culture. The Chatham Island Forget-me-not more resembles a hydrangea with its rich heads of blue

Right "*There are few plants more rewarding than Archangelica officinalis, with its almost spherical heads of flowers*"

Below *In spring the Fritillaria imperialis shows its yellow or burnt umber flowers. The Crown Imperial, in the legend, is said to have stared too boldly at Jesus Christ, and to have had to hang its flower heads, ever since, in shame*

Opposite above *Lupins rear their brightly coloured spires of flowers, while overhead floats a cloud of the blossom of Crambe cordifolia, which not only has spectacular flowers, but huge heart shaped leaves as well*

Below left *Helleborus corsicus has massed heads of jade green flowers in early spring, and richly sculpted leaves. It is the finest of all the hellebores*

Below right *Digitalis. The Excelsior strains of foxglove have eye catching flowers in brighter shades of pink and cream as well as mauve, and differ from the type in that their upturned flowers are arranged all round the stem, instead of only on one side*

flowers and corrugated leaves. It likes a
cool damp position in acid soil, and a lot
of water in dry weather. It responds
gratefully to a dressing of fish manure.

Onopordon (*Compositae*) These decorative thistles are valuable for their almost
pure white, fiercely spined leaves, and
noble branching habit of growth. O.
arabicum can reach ten feet, O. Acanthium (the Scotch Thistle) seldom tops
five. Both are prolific seeders.

Phormium (*Liliaceae*) Phormium tenax
– the New Zealand Flax, does well in all
but the severest climates. It will grow in
any good soil, but appreciates watering
in dry spells. It looks well by water.
P. variegatum has leaves that are parti-
coloured in green and yellow. The rarer
P. atropurpureum is much prized.

Verbascum (*Scrophulariaceae*) There
are many verbascums which are valuable
for their soaring height and candelabra of
golden (and occasionally, pink or white)
flowers. The best are V. Chaixii, a ten
foot biennial with splendid branching
flower heads. The perennial Pink Domino,
white Miss Willmott, sulphur yellow
Gainsborough, or clear yellow, purple-
eyed Vernale, are all good plants. For
the rock garden, there is V. spinosum, a
distinct and desirable shrublet seldom
more than ten inches.

Yucca (*Liliaceae*) That great gardener
Gertrude Jekyll called the yucca the
noblest plant in the garden. Y. gloriosa
(Adam's Needle) lives up to its name,
though Y. filamentosa flowers more
regularly. Y. variegata is a rare and
tropical looking plant, with leaves striped
with yellow.

*Topiary, surely the most architectural of
any feature of the garden not of brick or
stone, is shown to advantage in three
garden views*
Left *Clipped cypresses in the great
Californian garden of Filoli, San Mateo*
Opposite above *Clipped yews surround
a fountain in the famous National Trust
garden of Nymans in Sussex*
Below *Shaven box makes a maze-like
pattern in a garden in Italy*

Naturalizing

The art of natural gardening consists, in the words of the great William Robinson, of planting plants - whether trees, shrubs, or flowers - which, once set, will look after themselves.

Natural or "wild" gardening, like water-gardening is a new idea. Though the English invented the landscape garden (and it has been called their one great contribution to the visual arts), it was not until a hundred years later that gardeners gave serious thought to planting interesting trees and shrubs and flowers, where they would naturalize and present beautiful pictures. Capability Brown's choice of trees was limited - though, with the new importations from the Far East and America, less limited than that of his predecessor, William Kent, who was without the rhododendron, the magnolia, and many of the maples, to use as material to create his "opening and retiring shades" as Horace Walpole described the glades at Rousham.

And the great landscape gardeners of the eighteenth century did not create their "vistos" and bosky thickets of what we today would consider very interesting shrubs and trees - cedars and "immemorial elms" apart. They seldom thought of naturalizing flowers. The idea of simulating, and going one better than nature, by planting drifts of daffodils in grass, or contriving plantings of snowdrops and aconites under trees, came much later.

"All gardens," Hugh Farmar has written, "are the result of man's artifice. But careful grouping distinguishes the natural garden from both the formal and the wild garden. For a wild garden, though it should contain plants and shrubs in agreeable association, is essentially without form. The natural garden, on the other hand, has a definite plan that allows it to be enjoyed as a whole, as well as in detail." And Mr Farmar believes that the natural garden has a great future, because it appeals to ingenuity probably involves less expense and labour to lay out, and certainly less to maintain. It is but another form of landscape gardening

Above *"A primrose by a river's brim, a yellow primrose was to him." Him, being the dullard Peter Bell in Wordsworth's poem. But for most of us Primula vulgaris means the very spring itself*

Opposite *Under ideal circumstances, the Natural Garden should blend into its surroundings, and man-made plantings in the foreground lead the eye to distances beyond. Natural gardening on the grandest scale at Ripley House in County Kerry, Eire*

on a grander scale as practised in the eighteenth century.

But in natural gardening, as in all forms of gardening, certain rules have to be observed. The object to be borne in mind is to emulate Nature as closely as possible. Do not introduce rock work if you live in a part of the country where there is no natural stone. If your soil is strongly alkaline, avoid the labour, expense, and strain of importing peaty soil for a plantation of azaleas. Elsewhere, the point has been made that in nature, plants of one kind are apt to grow in groups. "And the eye, unconsciously perhaps, welcomes similar groupings in a garden. Much greater effect can be achieved by a generous grouping of simple things, than by a scattering of single plants, however rare and beautiful."

It is in the power of the talented natural gardener to create garden pictures as beautiful as any that can be found in a herbaceous border, or even more beautiful, because they look natural. Nothing could be more telling than a drift of crocus under the infant crimson leaves of a Japanese Maple, or, of the blue flowers of Anemone appenina under the white, blossom-laden branches of the elegant Prunus Shimidzu-Sakura, or the arching Shirotae. And such garden pictures are to be conjured at all seasons, not only in spring. Even in the depths of winter, when the rest of the garden is fast asleep, the coloured stems of the Siberian cornus, gold or lacquer red, and the barks of some maples, in association with the warm russet of dead leaves or bracken, can wonderfully cheer the eye. And there are sensational planting combinations to be made in autumn, too, with mauve Autumn Crocus, and the flaming leaves of the Turkey Oak, or with the lucent fruits of Viburnum opulus. All these planted pictures, once planted, need no care to speak of. What further proof is needed that natural gardening is the most practical form of gardening for today?

Above *Anemone japonica, unlike most anemones, flowers in late summer, and the white form is the most attractive. Honorine Jobert is a good form. Japanese anemones are useful plants for town gardeners, and will quickly settle down and naturalize in shady city plots. They prefer damp soil, with some peat in it, and are to be propagated by root cuttings*

Opposite *A sylvan corner by the lake in the garden at Wakehurst in Sussex, which has recently become an annexe of the world famous garden at Kew. Specimen trees planted informally reflect their greens in the water, while the fallen flowers of a lofty Rhododendron loderi King George lay a scented carpet. In the background, the pale gold of Acer japonicum aureum*

Acer (*Aceraceae*) Of the huge family of maples these are a few of the best to grow – A. japonicum aureum, with golden leaves, A. palmatum, the Japanese Maple, A. dissectum atropurpureum, with purple leaves, A. negundo variegatum, with white variegated leaves and A. pseudoplatanus brilliantissimum, with pink young foliage in spring.

Anemone (*Ranunculaceae*) The anemones, the name of which is unchanged since the days of Theophrastus (371–287 BC) are amongst the most beautiful of flowers for naturalizing, and some are among the earliest of spring flowers. A. appenina shows large blue daisy flowers, and likes some shade. A. blanda has flowers of deeper blue. The wild A. nemorosa makes broad clumps in moist woodland. Some forms of this, such as A. allenii, are flushed pale pink.

Anemone vulgaris, now known more usually as Anemone pulsatilla, could not be more ineptly named, as there is nothing vulgar about its appearance; in fact it is one of the most elegant and refined – both in flower and leaf, of any plant one knows. More romantically named, in English, Pasque Flower, the blue form Budapest is one of the loveliest, while the handsome rubra is a deep rosy pink. The pulsatillas need sharp drainage, and do well on chalk.

Japanese anemones (A. japonica) Both pink and white forms of Japanese anemones flower in late summer and are tolerant of town conditions, if given a peaty soil and moist situation. Honorine Jobert is one of the best white forms.

Camassia (*Liliaceae*) The Quamash is a good lily-like plant for naturalizing, and the famous gardener, Miss Ellen

Above right *Camellias and daffodils naturalized by a stream in Hampshire*
Below *Rhododendron arboreum can grow to a height of twenty feet, and bears its handsome heads of flowers in early spring*
Opposite *Drifts of different narcissus catch the sun in the garden of Hush Heath Manor, a house in Kent which dates from Tudor times*

Willmott, is said to have planted several thousand of them. C. leichtlinii, with flowers of white, purple, or blue, is the best.

Chionodoxa (*Liliaceae*) There are several lesser known species chionodoxas which are quite as attractive as the well known blue Glory of the Snow. C. Luciliae rosea is pink; C. cretica is blue and white; while the seldom grown C. grandiflora is mauve.

Colchicum (*Liliaceae*) The Autumn Crocus have a strange, slightly sinister, charm of their own. They belong to the lily family – unlike ordinary crocuses, which are iridaceae. There are many good new hybrids, such as the violet Autumn Queen, Violet Queen, and the large flowered Water-Lily.

Cornus (*Cornaceae*) There are many Dogwoods, some of the easiest culture, some more difficult. For the connoisseurs there are C. florida, the American Dogwood, which seldom flowers as well in Britain as it does in America. Apple Blossom and Cherokee Chief are good ones to look for: C. Kousa, from Japan, with cream-white flowers, tinged with rose, borne along its horizontally growing branches in May, colours well in autumn: Cornus Mas is the yellow flowered, red berried Cornelian Cherry, and C. nuttallii is a vigorous grower with white flowers touched with pink. Easier plants, but first class doers, are the well-known

Above right *Rhododendron Macabeanum from Manipur, in India, with large, pale-ribbed leaves and clustered flowers of rich yellow*
Below *Two great rhododendrons for gardeners on acid soil, scarlet R. shilsoni, and the paler flowered R. arboreum. Both flower early in spring, while the oak trees' branches are still bare*
Opposite *A cherry tree, with daffodils growing in rough grass – classic example of Natural Gardening. Here Prunus sargentii subhirtella Accolade shows its hanging bouquets of pale pink flowers and coppery spring foliage, with clumps of daffodils and narcissus below*

C. alternifolia argentea, with variegated leaves; C. sibirica, with sealing wax red stems, if cut down yearly; and C. stolonifera flaviramea, with yellow stems.

Crocus (*Iridaceae*) Crocuses are the ideal plants for naturalizing – indeed, unless they are grown in pots, they can hardly be grown in any other way. Some of the species crocuses are particularly attractive. A few for the discerning gardener would include the sweet smelling Scotch Crocus, Crocus biflorus, cream marked with purple; the orange chrysanthus; the lilac thomasinianus; and the large flowered white or purple vernus. Of the many beautiful seedlings and hybrids raised from these, Crocus biflorus weldenii Fairy, chrysanthus Blue Pearl, and deep orange chrysanthus E. A. Bowles, and the unusual, almost dark blue, C. vernus Naval Guard are quite outstanding.

Cyclamen (*Primulaceae*) The hardy cyclamen can provide flowers as well as

Five kinds of Wind Flowers or anemone, the name by which Theophrastus described them more than two thousand years ago

Top *Anemone pulsatilla – the Pasque Flower, "one of the most elegant and refined in flower and leaf of any plant one knows"*

Centre left *Anemone nemorosa – the white or pale pink anemone of the woodland*

Centre right *Anemone appenina, with large blue daisy flowers*

Bottom left *A beautiful form of A. pulsatilla – A.p. rubra, shows its rosy flowers in early spring. All the pulsatilla anemones like full sun and sharp drainage, and, preferably, a chalky soil*

Bottom right *A darker blue form of Anemone blanda*

Opposite *In a garden of rare trees in Hampshire, the spectacular Chilean Fire Bush, Embothrium coccineum shows its brilliant flowers in May. The Fire Bush was introduced to Western gardens by William Lobb in 1846. It likes an acid soil and a mild climate, as does the tree beyond, the yellow leaved maple, Acer cappadocicum*

Opposite left *Four beautiful magnolias – Magnolia stellata, the lowest growing of all magnolias. It grows slowly but has an attractively mature look from its earliest youth*

Above right *Magnolia soulangiana, one of the most perennially popular of all magnolias, has the advantage for gardeners on alkaline soil of tolerating some lime*

Below left *The rosy flowered M. soulangiana lennei is the earliest to bloom, so its flowers are liable to damage by frost*

Below right *The lily flowered M. liliflora nigra has dark purple flowers, and is a hearty grower*

Right *Camassia leichtlinii, a good plant for naturalizing, will soon form sizeable colonies. Camassia or Quamash, to give it its N. American Indian name, comes in white, purple or blue forms*

the most delightful marbled foliage, for many months of the year. C. atkinsii flowers through January to March, C. repandum and C. coum from March till April, C. europaeum flowers from August to October, as does the popular C. neapolitanum.

Eucryphia (*Eucryphiaceae*) For gardens on non-calcareous soil the eucryphias are some of the most beautiful and rewarding of trees. By far the best are that great hybrid, Nymansay (child of the delicate E. glutinosa and evergreen cordifolia, and combining the qualities of both) and the newer Rostrevor, with flowers like white anemones.

Fothergilla (*Hamamelidaceae*) The fothergillas all have flowers like miniature bottle-bushes in spring and bright autumn colouring. They dislike heavy soil and lime. F. monticola Huntsman is the best, and it colours brilliantly.

Galanthus (*Amaryllidaceae*) Even the most captious connoisseur would be hard put to it to find a snowdrop more desirable to naturalize in his garden than the ordinary Galanthus nivalis: but G. Elwesii is larger and the attractive green markings on its petals more pronounced.

Galtonia (*Liliaceae*) Also known as Hyacinthus candicans, the Spire Lilies are the most useful bulbous plants, as they produce their spring-like white flowers in late summer. They will naturalize well in the front of shrubberies in open sunshine, or light shade, and their flowers are slightly fragrant.

Genista (*Leguminosae*) The broom was the flower of the Plantagenets (Plante à Genêt) and there are several genistas which are kingly plants for the garden or shrubbery. The low growing G. hispanica, the Spanish Gorse, makes a compact dark green bush covered with golden flowers in May and June; G. lydia shows its yellow flowers at the same time. The new G. tinctoria Royal Gold flowers a little later, as does the Mount Etna Broom, G. aethnensis, which can make an elegant tree covered with flowers in July and August.

Gentiana (*Gentianaceae*) The gentians' very name is synonymous with blue. The best varieties for the discriminating gardener are G. acaulis, with brilliant blue trumpet flowers and evergreen mats of leaves; the Willow Gentian, G. asclepiadea, taller, with dark blue flowers on two-foot stems in late summer, a particularly good plant for naturalizing in the front of the shrub-border; the eye-catching, free flowering, but lime-hating, hybrid, Macaulayi, which flowers in September; and G. septemfida, good natured and generous in flower. G. sino-ornata grows well in soil rich in leaf mould and can flower till Christmas. The best loved gentian of all, G. verna, flowers, as its name implies, in spring.

Kalmia (*Ericaceae*) Lucky is the gardener whose garden is on the acid soil suitable for growing kalmias. All are connoisseurs' plants, though perhaps K. latifolia Brilliant and K. l. Clementine Churchill are the two most desirable. It is often thought that kalmias, like rhododendrons like some shade, but they prefer full sun, and a moist soil.

Magnolia (*Magnoliaceae*) How lucky for the modern gardener that Monsieur Magnol, director, two hundred years ago, of the Botanical Garden at Montpellier, had such a graceful name to give to some of the most graceful of all trees. He might have been called Schmidt.

All magnolias like good soil, shelter from spring frosts, and partial shade. Of all things, being woodland trees in the wild, they like a mulch of dead leaves) Some magnolias (M. Kobus, for instance

are more tolerant of lime than others.

Magnolias for the connoisseur would certainly include the splendid M. grandi-flora exoniensis, the Exmouth magnolia, with huge globe-like flowers in late summer; M. parviflora, with red stamened flowers in May and June; M. soulangiana lennei, with purple flowers in spring; the delicate dusky flowered M. s. nigra; the sweet smelling M. stellata, a low growing magnolia, which takes many years to reach a height of four feet; and lastly, aristocrat among aristocrats, but a plant only for the patient gardener, with perfect growing conditions to offer, and a gentle climate, M. Campbellii from the East Himalayas, a tree of pyramidal shape, glaucous leaves, and, after twenty years, the most beautiful rose-coloured flowers in very early spring.

Narcissus (*Amaryllidaceae*) Daffodils (Narcissus pseudo-narcissus) and what are generally called narcissus, are the naturalizing plants par excellence. They have been immensely developed in recent years and some of the new hybrids are much larger, showier and more sophis-ticated, if perhaps less poetically beautiful than the simple Lent Lilies from which most of them derive. Wordsworth would have been surprised by the host of new white, lemon coloured and even pink-tinged daffodils – as well as golden – which grow in modern gardens. Of these new flowers a few are outstanding: some of the best of the golden are Golden Harvest, Hunters Moon, the old favourite King Alfred and the mimosa-coloured Rembrandt. Some of the most effective bi-coloured daffodils are Ballygarvy, General Patton and the white petalled,

Left *Lush planting by the waterside in a Berkshire garden. Through the mixed foliage, and reflected in the water, is the glint of astilbes*
Opposite *Hydrangea macrophylla in the foreground, and a fine specimen of yellow flowered Genista aethnensis beyond. The Etna Broom is a particularly useful plant, as it casts little shade, and so can be effectively underplanted*

yellow trumpeted Spring Glory. The elegant Beersheba, Cantatrice and Mrs E. Krelage have white trumpets.

Narcissus have been even more sensationally developed than daffodils. A few of the most striking are Carlton, with soft yellow perianths and finely goffered crowns, Tinker (its growers describe it as "a charming flower with a sunny disposition"), yellow and vivid red, and Chinese White, pure white; while Double Event and Golden Ducat are fully double with flowers as furbelowed as dahlias.

All these newcomers are very splendid, but perhaps for the connoisseur the old species narcissus have more appeal.

Above *Kalmia latifolia, the Mountain Laurel or Calico Bush originates in Eastern North America. It has pink chintzy flowers*
Left above *Lunaria annua – or old-fashioned Honesty, is an attractive plant for growing in the wilder parts of the garden and the dried seed pods make effective indoor decoration*
Below *Mahonia japonica shows handsome pinnate evergreen leaves and sweet smelling pale yellow flowers in earliest spring*
Opposite *An informal planting of rhododendrons and azaleas with a well-placed urn beyond, to catch and hold the eye*

Flowers such as the quaint Bulbocodium conspicuus, (large trumpet – hardly any perianth), so suitably named the Hoop Petticoat Narcissus, the miniature N. cyclamineus, such as the twin flowered Tête à Tête, and tough little Peeping Tom. But perhaps the prettiest of the lot is Narcissus triandrus, descriptively known as Angel's Tears.

Paulownia (*Scrophulariaceae*) Paulownia originates in China, and was introduced in the forties of the last century and named for a green-fingered Russian Grand Duchess who became Queen of Holland. It succeeds in light sandy loam and a sheltered position, but sometimes its beautiful blue foxglove-like flowers (the buds of which are formed in autumn) are cut by spring frosts. For gardeners in search of fine foliage, one way of cultivating paulownia is to prune its branches back to within a few inches of their base – the leaves it then produces are gigantic, though the flowers are lost. P. tomentosa imperialis is the kind to look for.

Polyanthus (*Primulaceae*) These are almost too well known to need description, but how many gardeners know that polyanthus is a man-made plant, and was first produced in the seventeenth century, as a result of crossing the ordinary primrose and cowslip? In latter years many spectacular new strains of polyanthus have been produced, some with flowers of blue and pink, colours quite new to polyanthus. The Munstead Strain, raised by Miss Gertrude Jekyll shows the most delicate range of shades of cream, yellow, orange, and white.

Primula (*Primulaceae*) Primulas make ideal plants for naturalizing in woodland or by the waterside. They all like a deep acid soil and above all, moisture. A few for the connoisseur are the apricot yellow Bulleyana, the yellow scented Florindae, P. japonica Miller's Crimson, and the rose coloured rosea Delight.

But however Delightful and however Crimson there is no primula as eternally touching as the woodland primrose. "A primrose by a river's brim, a yellow primrose was to him." Him, being the dullard Peter Bell in Wordsworth's poem. But for the most of us Primula vulgaris means the very spring itself.

Prunus (*Rosaceae*) How does any gardener make his pick of the immense family of prunus at his disposal? Perhaps he should look for habit of growth and autumn colouring, as much as for generosity and brilliance of flower in what can be a short flowering season. Four he would choose certainly are P. Blireiana with its coppery leaves, double pink flowers, and handsome bearing; P. Accolade (sargentii subhirtella) for its hanging clusters of pink flowers in April; the fastigiate Amanagawa (lannesiana erecta) for its unique columnar growth; P. subhirtella, for its welcome gift of flowering in mid-winter. Other prunus of great beauty are Hisakura (better than the too-often planted Kansan), the pale pink Hokusai, the elegantly shaped Shimidzu Sakura, with pure white

39

wreaths of flowers, Shirotae, also white, but of an almost weeping habit, the dazzling Tai Haku (the Great White Cherry), and the unusual yellow Ukon, of which the leaves turn a dark red in autumn. But perhaps if there was room in the garden for only one prunus, the thoughtful gardener's choice would fall on P. sargentii, a tree of splendid form, splendid flower, and splendid autumn colouring.

Rhododendron (*Ericaceae*) For gardens on acid soil, especially if they partly consist of woodland, rhododendrons or azaleas offer a very special world of plants. Out of the thousands of species and hybrids available, a few for the connoisseur should surely include the following. Hybrid Rhododendrons: Christmas Cheer, Essex Scarlet, Gomer Waterer, Kluis Sensation, Madame Carvalho, nobleanum, Sappho, Stella Waterer – all

of the easiest culture. Others are Blue Diamond, Blue Tit, Britannia, Conroy, Crest, Doncaster, fragrantissimum (for the greenhouse), Goldsworth Yellow, Hawk, Kilimanjaro, Lady Bessborough, Lady Chamberlain, loderi King George, Mother of Pearl, Penjerrick, Polar Bear (for its July flowering), praecox, shilsoni, Tally-Ho. A few of the most rewarding species rhododendrons are: arboreum, Augustinii, bullatum, calophytum, campylocarpum, cinnabarinum, concatenans (for its curiously scented leaves), Falconeri, Griersonianum, griffithianum, Macabeanum, mucronatum, orbiculare, sinogrande, and Thomsonii.

Smilacina (*Liliaceae*) The False Spikenards originate in North America and Sikkim. They look well if planted in moist loam in shady woodland or in the front of shrub-borders, where their white flowers and bright green foliage are particularly fresh looking and pleasing. S. racemosa is the form usually grown.

Spartium (*Leguminosae*) The Spanish Broom provides bright yellow flowers in late summer and succeeds in full sun. It is useful for clothing dry banks, and for planting in sea-side gardens. Hard pruning (short of the old woody growth) prevents the shrub from becoming too tall and spindly.

Syringa (*Oleaceae*) The lilacs have wafted their scent round Western gardens for centuries, the hybrids and cultivars of the original S. vulgaris being among the best known and best loved small trees we have. A few of the very best are the mauve pink Katherine Havemeyer, the snowy Madame Lemoine, and the violet-red, late flowering Mrs Edward Harding. These three are double. Single lilacs to look for, are the favourite Souvenir de Louis Spaeth (wine red), Marechal Foch (carmine), and the pale yellow Primrose, which first surprised Western gardeners in 1949.

Less well known, but equally desirable lilacs are the bone-hardy Preston Hybrids raised by Miss Isabella Preston in Canada: the rose-pink Bellicent and pale lilac Elinor are two of the best. Two more lilacs for the connoisseur are the small leaved, low growing S. microphylla superba, which flowers on and off throughout the summer, and the miniature Korean Lilac, S. velutina (or Palibiniana), which flowers well even when quite young. The modest size of S. velutina makes it a most useful plant for the smaller gardens of today.

Tiarella (*Saxifragaceae*) Tiarella wherryi is the best of the group, and presents its white foamy flowers above neat clusters

Right *Hemerocallis have been immensely improved by hybridization in the last few years and are now to be had in different shades of pink, amber and maroon as well as the accustomed orange and yellow*

Below *Agapanthus naturalized near an Acer japonicum, with wine-red leaves. The new Headbourne Hybrid agapanthus – reared in Hampshire, far away from their native South Africa, have proved quite hardy in gardens that are not too cold*

Opposite *Genista aetnensis, the elegant Mount Etna broom presents an almost Oriental outline and rich yellow flowers in late summer. In the border beyond grows a handsome clump of Achillea Gold Plate*

of leaves in spring. It looks well if planted in woodland or light shade.

Trillium (*Liliaceae*) The white American Wood Lily is a true connoisseur's plant, and has the rare look of all flowers with only three petals: but it must have the conditions it likes – moist, leafy soil, in woodland shade. The purple flowered variety, T. erectum, has less appeal.

Viburnum (*Caprifoliaceae*) The viburnums comprise some of the most valuable of all shrubs or small trees. A short list for the gardener in search of the very best, might include V. betulifolium, of which the branches are bowed down with scarlet fruit in autumn; the scented winter flowering bodnantense (a cross between fragrans and grandiflorum); V. Carlcephalum with its huge clusters of headily scented flowers in May; the glaucous leaved V. cylindricum; the dioecious V. Davidi, which needs to be planted with another of the opposite sex before it produces its enchanting blue berries; the autumn flowering V. fragrans; the sweet smelling Juddii; the autumn colouring Lentago; the apricot fruited V. nudum; the impressive, shade-loving, evergreen rhytidophyllum; the Lanarth variety of V. tomentosum and the magnificent V. tomentosum Mariesii, both of which have their white flowers strung along their horizontally growing branches in a taking and delightful way. V. t. Mariesii is a degree less robust than the excellent Lanarth.

Left above *Mahonia Charity, a cross between M. lomariifolia and M. japonica, is an early spring flowerer. It bears erect its sweetly-scented racemes of flowers, and seldom exceeds a height of ten feet*
Below *Erica alpina, a Tree Heath which makes a dense, sweetly scented bush up to nine feet high – E. alpina is hardier (as might be expected from its name) than the more usually planted E. arborea. Its foliage is a vivid and pleasing green*
Opposite *A bank closely covered with a natural planting of different ericas. Some of the best of these – the Erica carnea group, will put up with some lime in the soil*

Foliage

Above *The giant form of Petasites fragrans or Winter Heliotrope, an impressive foliage plant for a damp place, but a rampant spreader*

Opposite *A beautiful tree for gardeners on acid soil. Davidia involucrata, the Dove, or more prosaically Handkerchief Tree. Its large white bracts, hanging from inconspicuous flowers, are unusually attractive. It was named for the Abbé David (1826–1900) who sent back many excellent plants from China in the last century*

The leaf or the flower? Lately the thoughtful gardener has come to value the leaf more highly - not perhaps more highly than the flower, but more highly than he did. After all, leaves last longer than flowers. For months on end they are the furniture of the garden, giving it form and a feeling of composition and permanence. Plants with fine foliage or - better still - coloured leaves, if grouped with the fleeting flowers of tulips, wallflowers, or even roses, can give a garden a more lively look and a subtler colour scheme. It can be said that fine foliage makes fine borders, but it gives a garden something more, that indefinable but all-important quality which is so difficult to attain, especially in young gardens - character.

For the botanist, of course, the leaves of a plant have always been important, and have served, even more than the flowers, to identify the plant in question. The tongue-twisting corymbulosus, rhytidophyllus, and odontophyllus tell us, merely, that the plant has clustered, wrinkled, or tooth-edged leaves. "Why," the learned Professor Earle has asked, "should we allow a pile of heterogeneous names to stand as a barrier . . . the strange names are all but barren of interest in themselves: what interest they possess springs wholly out of the objects they represent" - that is, differing, wrinkled, tooth-edged, or whatever. Ruskin disapproved of the latinization of plant names, and resented the fact that some nuts should be described as having petals like those of pinks, and some pinks as having petals like nuts. So did Rousseau, and he resented the fact that the answer to a simple inquiry as to the name of a flower should take the form of "a long tirade of Latin names which sounds like a conjuration of hobgoblins". He might, as the author of this book once wrote elsewhere, have preferred the name of Old Man to artemisia and Sow Bread to cyclamen.

Recently a host of good foliage plants have caught and held

the attention of the gardener of taste. Plants which were seldom planted in the flower garden fifty years ago, or if they were, were relegated to the herb garden or kitchen garden.

Such plants as the blue-leaved rue, Ruta graveolens (graveolens means strongly scented), and the golden leaved balm (Melissa aurea), which were once grown only in olitories, now have honoured places in the blue or golden border. Quite ordinary shrubs such as elaeagnus, euonymus, and even the dowdy golden privet, take on new importance if planted where their bright leaves can light up the garden scene. There are prunus and perilla and Rhus cotinus to give rich tones of red; the glaucous Fescue Grass (Festuca glauca) and ruta to provide blue; artemisia (or, to please Rousseau - Old Man) senecio and phlomis for silver and grey. Cineraria maritima shows leaves that are frosty white, and Actinidia kolomikta has leaves that look as if they were splashed with pink and white paint. On these pages, accent is on plants with coloured leaves; plants of architectural form are discussed elsewhere.

Artemisia (*Compositae*) The artemisias have several colloquial names, being known as Southern Wood, Wormwood, or, indiscriminately, Old Man and Old Woman. Their silvery foliage can be one of the beauties of the border in late summer. Some of the best are Lambrook Silver, Silver Queen, and A. versicolor, which has curled leaves. A. Palmeri is a fine plant but a rampant spreader. One of the few artemisias which will be happy in moist shade is the green leafed, cream flowered A. lactiflora.

Atriplex (*Chenopodiaceae*) There are two atriplex well worth growing. A. Halimus, which makes a fine silvery leaved shrub, especially in seaside gardens, and A. hortensis, the Red Orach, a red-leaved annual, and an excellent border plant, if leaf colour is looked for.

Ballota (*Labiatae*) A grey foliage plant much used in Europe for bedding out schemes, but seldom used in colder climates because it is not quite hardy, and impatient of damp. It looks well in tubs or vases planted with white and pink geraniums. If grown by itself it benefits from a light clipping in August.

Berberis (*Berberidaceae*) Of the huge family of barberrys, favourites are B. thunbergii atropurpurea, with deep claret-coloured leaves, and the dwarf, B. nana. B. Wilsonae has particularly fine coral berries. Rosy Glow shows pink young foliage in spring. Barbarossa berries magnificently. B. telomaica, from Tibet, is a seldom grown, almost blue leaved, berberis, which can grow to six or seven feet.

Right above *The variegated form of Lunaria annua or Honesty, shows fresh green, cream flaked leaves*

Below *Hosta Sieboldiana, right, is one of the most beautiful of the Plantain Lilies. Its leaves are glaucous blue and great ground coverers. Left, the white and green dappled leaves of Scrophularia nodosa variegata, the Knotted Figwort*

Opposite *A group of finely contrasting foliage with a mass of Cineraria maritima in the foreground, and the sword-like leaves of Yucca gloriosa above*

Bocconia (*Papaveraceae*) The Plume Poppies are imposing plants for the back of a mixed border or in groups in the shrubbery. Their glaucous green foliage has been likened to giant aces of clubs and they raise spires of cream coloured flowers in July. Also known as macleaya.

Brassica (*Cruciferae*) Cabbages would seem unexpected plants to recommend to connoisseurs but the Decorative Kale, Brassica acephala variegata, with its multi-coloured leaves is a splendid plant for foliage-fans.

Bupleurum (*Umbelliferae*) For some reason, this excellent shrub, with faintly glaucous leaves and yellow umbels of flowers is not often grown, though it is quite hardy; it especially thrives near the sea.

Cineraria maritima (*Compositae*) This has handsome deeply cut leaves which are almost white. It flourishes by the sea, and in poor soil and full sunlight. It is hardy only in the mildest climates and is best raised every year from cuttings. Its

Left *A border planted with an eye to the value of differing leaf forms. In the near corner Bergenia cordifolia, with iris beyond. In or out of flower the yellow daisied shrub, Senecio Greyii shows soft silver leaves. The floribunda rose is the popular Iceberg*

Opposite above left *The bluish, pungent leaves of Ruta graveolens, Jackmans Blue with yellow flowers, and alchemilla*

Above right *The young scarlet foliage of Pieris forrestii is as brilliant as any flower, and at its best in early spring. The flowers of pieris are like Lily of the Valley, and smell as sweet*

Bottom left *Silver leaved Senecio Greyii, in the front with Bocconia cordata, the Plume Poppy, behind. In between, Torch Lilies, or Red Hot Pokers, to light the scene*

Bottom right *A real plant for the connoisseur Myosoitidium nobile, the Chatham Island Forget-me-Not, with its blue heads of flowers and richly corrugated leaves. It likes a damp position and a diet of fish manure*

yellow daisy flowers are undistinguished and better snipped off.

Davidia (*Cornaceae*) Abbé David (1826–1900) sent back many plants and trees from China during his time there as a missionary, but none more beautiful than Davidia involucrata, the Dove, or more prosaically, Handkerchief Tree, called after the striking white leaf bracts which surround its inconspicuous flowers in May. Davidia will thrive in any good soil, but is slow to flower.

Elaeagnus (*Elaeagnaceae*) The elaeagnus are a useful, workaday lot, but the evergreen E. ebbingei is an excellent hedge making plant for seaside gardeners. E. pungens aureovariegata – though far from rare, has as brilliant foliage of green and gold as any evergreen, and E. p. variegata has leaves splashed with cream.

Euonymus (*Celastraceae*) Euonymus alatus, with its corky bark and oriental line is spectacular, and E. fortunei gracilis, with its silver variegated foliage, and half trailing, half clinging habit is a most useful and attractive plant. E. ovatus aureus has showy leaves which are splashed with yellow, especially when planted in a sunny position.

Hippophae (*Elaeagnaceae*) Hippophae rhamnoides, the Sea Buck Thorn, has cheerful silver foliage and a mass of orange berries which are too bitter for the hungriest bird to eat. Plants of different sexes, one male to six females – should

Right above *In the corner of a well planted bed are cushions of silver leaved santolina, or Cotton Lavender with the spreading claret coloured leaves of Rheum palmatum, a garden form of rhubarb, behind. Santolina looks better if given a hard clipping back each spring*

Below *Euonymus fortunei gracilis "with its silver variegated foliage, and half trailing, half clinging habit, is a most useful and attractive plant". Its leaves are sometimes tinged with pink*

Opposite *The sharp leaves of Crocosmia masonorum, with orange, montbretia-like, flowers contrast with rhododendrons. Crocosmia is a good plant for naturalizing*

be planted near enough to each other to make pollenization possible. Hippophae does well by the sea.

Lunaria (*Cruciferae*) The annual Honesty is perhaps not worth growing except as a foliage plant in its less common variegated form; but its seed heads are useful, if dried for winter decoration.

Mahonia (*Berberidaceae*) There are several mahonias which are well worthy of the connoisseur. Mahonia Aquifolium Charity, with lemon yellow flowers in earliest spring, the exotic leaved M. lomariifolia, and almost best of all, the seldom grown M. Moseri, a small shrub with pink leaves in spring, changing to bright and then dark green as the season passes. All mahonias dislike being moved about.

Perilla (*Labiatae*) This is a decorative annual, worth growing for the striking effect of its dark bronze leaves, which associate well with plants of silver foliage.

Petasites (*Compositae*) The name petasites derives from the Greek petasos, a large hat and was given to the plant by Dioscorides. The only one worth growing is the giant-leaved form, but it should be planted where its rampant growth will not smother more delicate plants.

Phlomis (*Labiatae*) The two best of the

Left above *An imposing group of Bocconia cordata, in Oslo's Botanical Garden. The Plume Poppies' glaucous leaves have been likened to giant aces of clubs. Bocconia is also known as macleaya*

Below *Ballota, a grey leaved plant for gardeners in climates with mild winters. It grows readily from cuttings*

Opposite above *A corner of a garden with an oriental look. Many different leaf forms, supplied by hostas, ivies and maples, make a pleasing composition*

Below left *The silver silky haired leaves of Salvia argentea, one of the best of the great family of sages. It likes full sun and sharp drainage*

Below right *The boldly crinkled leaves of Veratrum nigrum. Veratrum thrives in any rich soil and likes plenty of moisture*

phlomis are still the well known P. fruticosa, the Jerusalem Sage, with silver velvety leaves and golden flowers each shaped like a miniature helmet, and P. italica, smaller with pinkish flowers. Phlomis like full sun and sharp drainage.

Pieris (*Ericaceae*) Lucky is the gardener on acid soil for he can grow pieris, some of the most beautiful and unusual of all shrubs. Unusual because their beauty lies in their young spring foliage rather than in their flowers.

Pieris Forest Flame (a cross between P. formosa forestii Wakehurst and P. japonica) is one of the best of all pieris. Three other first class shrubs are P. japonica Bert Chandler, from Australia, with young leaves of coral pink, the hardy P. j. Christmas Cheer and P. taiwanensis with outstanding sprays of white flowers in spring, and the striking spring foliage for which all pieris are noted.

Rheum (*Polygonaceae*) The ornamental rhubarbs show some of the largest leaves in the garden, and their flower heads are sensational in June. R. palmatum has green leaves and deep red flowers, but R. p. atropurpureum, with cream flowers and wine coloured foliage, is even more striking. They like to grow by, but not in, water.

Rhus (*Anacardiaceae*) Of the sumachs, the female form of Rhus typhina laciniata, with lacy, deeply divided leaves and fine autumn colouring is the one to look for. Rhus cotinus foliis purpureis (Notcutt's variety) is one of the very best of all red

Right above *Giant rosettes made by the flannelly leaves of Verbascum Chaixii, the grandest of all mulleins*
Below *Some of the Tibetan poppies, such as Meconopsis Wallichii, have fascinating foliage, especially in early spring, when their leaves are covered with golden down*
Opposite *Vines offer some of the most impressive leaves of any climbing plants and there are few with finer foliage than Vitis Coignetiae, especially if the purple leaved form is planted. In the foreground, the red tubular flowers of Fuchsia Thalia*

leaved shrubs. It should be pruned back each spring. Recently its name has been shortened to cotinus.

Ruta (*Rutaceae*) This is the foliage plant par excellence, and its striking blue leaves have earned it great popularity in recent years. The variegated form has an interesting appearance but is less attractive. Both should be pruned hard back in spring.

Salvia (*Labiatae*) Though "Red Salvias" may have a bad name, there are enough salvias, both herbaceous and shrubby, to make them one of the great plant families.

Taking the herbaceous ones first. The silken leaved S. argentea: S. superba (till recently S. virgata nemorosa) S. haematodes and the bright blue flowered S. uliginosa are fine plants, as is S. turkistanica with its hairy opalescent leaves and pungent flower spikes. The

Left *Senecio laxifolius is a shrub from New Zealand with grey felted leaves, which persist all year round, and a burst of yellow daisy flowers in summer. It is hardier than Senecio Greyii though similar. Senecio is a useful shrub for covering banks, as is shown here*

Opposite above left *Artemisia Palmeri makes slender spires of silver leaves in high summer, and can be grown in telling contrast to plants of darker foliage. It is rather spreading.*

Right *Phlomis fruticosa, the Jerusalem Sage, makes opulent mounds of grey leaves, surmounted by yellow flower heads in June. It is happiest in a hot dry position and likes some shelter*

Bottom left *Morina longifolia, with narrow thistly leaves and delicately modelled flowers of pink and white on erect stems, comes from the Himalayas, and is a border plant which is not often planted, though quite hardy*

Right *Onopordon Acanthium is one of the great garden thistles, with a soaring and vigorous habit and hoary leaves which are fiercely prickled. A biennial, it comes readily from seed and is one of the most imposing plants for the back of the border*

best of the shrubby salvias would include the purple form of the common sage S. purpurascens, the Painted Sage, S. tricolor with variegated leaves, and two beautiful but delicate plants S. Grahamii and S. Greggii, both with bright red flowers.

There are good annual sages too, such

Above left *Othonnopsis cheirifolia, with jade green, spatulate leaves is seen to advantage when grown by the edge of a low wall, or bank, where it can hang down and make a leafy curtain*

Above right *Sambucus nigra aurea is the invaluable Golden Elder, and few trees present such bright golden leaves throughout the season*

Below *The leaves of Stachys macrantha are a rich green, and adept at smothering weeds. In summer the plant is covered with full heads of purple flowers, which last well if cut*

Opposite above *Eryngium alpinum Donard is a good looking Sea Holly and has flowers like those of a teasel in shades of steely blue. But the real beauty of the plant is the involucres of fine filigree that surmount its stems*

Below *Rodgersia pinnata superba has fine leaves, like those of a giant chestnut, which redden as the season progresses. Rodgersia prefers a damp situation, and some shade*

Right *The new spring growth of some of the Himalayan rhododendrons is as spectacularly graceful as opening flowers*

as the eye-catching blue S. patens, the mealy stemmed S. farinacea, Blue Bedder, and the pink, white and purple leaved S. Horminum.

Santolina (*Compositae*) Lavender Cotton is one of the most popular of all silver leaved shrubs. S. Chamaecyparissus is the most often grown and responds well to clipping. S. neapolitana is an attractive variety with lighter, airier leaves and paler flowers. S. viridis has green leaves, and is a plant for those who like something different.

Sedum (*Crassulaceae*) There are several far better sedums to grow than the work-a-day S. spectabile. A new form, Brilliant, has brighter flowers which last longer – and S. Telephium Autumn Joy has handsome heads of long lasting crimson-bronze flowers. The red leaved form S. spectabile atropurpureum is another good sedum.

Senecio (*Compositae*) Of the shrubby senecios, one is quite outstanding, and though widely planted should still find a place in every garden, Senecio Greyii. Senecio clivorum, syn. Ligularia clivorum, is a handsome plant to plant by the waterside, with spreading leaves and shaggy yellow daisy flowers.

Skimmia (*Rutaceae*) The useful hardworking skimmias will grow equally well on chalk or acid soils, and their bright red berries are as cheerful as their glossy leaves. Two of the best to grow are S. Foremanii, and the finest fruiter of the group, is S. Reevesiana, which holds its berries through the winter.

Teucrium (*Labiatae*) The germanders offer silver foliage and misty, pale blue

Left above *Acanthus mollis has handsome leaves and an impressive sculptured form of growth. It is happy in full sun or some shade, and associates well with architecture*
Below *Of the many hebes with interesting leaves, the silver Hebe pageana, is one of the most attractive*
Opposite *A multi-coloured head of Decorative Kale, Brassica acephala variegata, surely one of the most showy vegetables of the garden*

flowers, but need protection in inland gardens. By the sea and in favoured climates they flourish. T. fruticans is the best variety. In Irish gardens teucrium is sometimes clipped into a low hedge.

Veratrum (*Liliaceae*) Veratrum makes a striking foliage plant in early summer when its clusters of deeply ribbed leaves are unfolding. V. nigrum is the one to grow. V. viride is the Indian Poke, with greenish-yellow flowers.

Scent

The doomed poet Shelley considered "the jessamine faint, and the sweet tuberose, the sweetest flower for scent that blows." The exotic tuberose (Polianthes tuberosa) and its culture is outside the scope of this book, but jasmine has spread its scent in Western gardens for years, and Milton linked it with the pink, the violet, the musk-rose and the pansy "freaked with jet" as among the sweetest of scented flowers.

Scent surely is one of the finest gifts of the garden. Many people love a particular plant for its scent alone. The new roses, they say - though it is not quite true - do not have the scent of the old ones. Lilies would still be beautiful, but sad, if they did not smell. Some plants, such as humea, the Incense Plant, and the seldom grown hot-house plant baronia, are in themselves plain-looking, and their flowers are insignificant - but their intoxicating scent endears them to us.

Much of the charm of herbs lies in their aromatic leaves. Some, such as lavender and rosemary, distil a perfume which is known and loved by all. Rosemary is always connected with remembrance, and is the perfect example of the nostalgia aroused by scent. In the past it was even considered medicinally to be good for the memory - the herbalist Gerard quoting "Arabian Physitions" as being of this opinion. Gerard also praised the rejuvenating qualities of rosemary: writing that even to smell its pungent leaves, kept one "youngly". Other herbs exude a sharper smell, and were used in old days for fumigating and hygienic purposes. The old French name for santolina (Cotton-lavender) was Guarde-Robe, as it was used as a deterrent for moths. Tansy, in the days of the early settlers in America, was used to freshen cupboards. Bacon advised the use of prostrate herbs, such as thyme, to make fragrant path-ways: "Therefore ye are to set whole alleys of them to have the pleasure when you walk or tread."

Above *Hybrid Tea rose Memoriam has petals that are tinged with pink at the heart* **Opposite** *Sweetly scented lily Imperial Crimson is a cross between auratum and speciosum. Below and to the right, lily Imperial Silver*

Boronia (*Rutaceae*) This remote relation of the rues is one of the most deliciously scented plants in the greenhouse. B. pinnata is the one to look for, but it will only be found in very special nurseries.

Buddleia (*Loganiaceae*) Most of the buddleias are strongly scented and a great attraction to bees and butterflies. A few of the best are Buddleia Fallowiana, with white felted leaves and strongly fragrant mauve flowers, Buddleia caryopteridifolia with woolly leaves and sweet smelling lavender flowers, Buddleia alternifolia – better as a free standing bush than against a wall, where its slender mauve sprays may be admired to the full: and several good varieties of Buddleia Davidi, such as the white Peace and pale blue Lochinch. Buddleia Colvilei is a real connoisseurs' plant, with unusually large rose-coloured drooping clusters of flowers; it needs a sheltered position as it is far from hardy; but it is a very beautiful plant.

Daphne (*Thymelaeaceae*) There are three daphnes which should be in every garden. D. Cneorum, miniature with pink flowers: D. Mezereum with strongly fragrant deep red flowers, and the May flowering pale pink D. burkwoodii, "Somerset".

Lavandula (*Labiatae*) There are very few lavenders which can be compared to the two most popular varieties – Lavandula officinalis, the old English Lavender, and L. vera, the Dutch lavender with slightly greyer leaves; but Folgate is considered by experts to be a better plant than the popular Munstead strain, and Hidcote is a specially rich purple. London Pink is an attractive pink-flowered form.

Left *That old favourite rose, Gloire de Dijon, has been scenting gardens for well over a century*
Below *The rich crimson flowers of Ena Harkness*
Opposite *Rosa moschata Buff Beauty makes a handsome shrub, with apricot coloured, apple-scented flowers over a long period. Its leaves are dark green and glossy*

Above *A rose garden with a Victorian air, but planted with the best of the modern floribundas such as the creamy white Dimples and deep pink Plentiful*
Opposite *The rose garden at historic Haddon Hall, once the home of the famous Dorothy Vernon. The pink flora-bunda rose in the foreground is Arakan*

Lilium (*Liliaceae*) Of this most beautiful race of flowers, there are just a few which should be in every lily-lover's garden. They have been chosen not only for their looks and scent, but also for their good nature and ease of culture.

"Wild" or species lilies Tigrinum, the Tiger Lily, regale, auratum, speciosum

(Shuksan and Cinderella), umbellatum (Golden Chalice).

Hybrid lilies The Aurelian hybrids, especially Black Dragon, Green Dragon, Golden Clarion and Limelight, Imperial Crimson and Imperial Silver.

Mid-Century hybrids Brandy Wine, Tabasco, Mountaineer, Prosperity, and

Above *The incomparable modern flori-bunda Iceberg with ice-white, subtly scented flowers. If only lightly pruned it will soon make a graceful shrub*

Right *Floribunda rose Amberley sheds its petals on the grass*

Opposite above *Musk roses such as the pink budded Cornelia and cream white, lemon centred Pax are among the most strongly perfumed of all roses, and flower for several months on end*

Below left *Peace – one of the greatest of modern roses, has splendid flowers. Faintly scented, and wonderfully healthy foliage*

Right *To curtain a wall with clear pink, sweet smelling flowers there are few roses like Madame Gregoire Staechlin (Spanish Beauty). It was raised in Spain and is the child of Frau Karl Druschki and Château de Clos Vougeot*

the vivid red Enchantment.

Turks Cap Lilies Martagon alba, mon-adelphum, cernuum, chalcedonicum.

Lonicera (*Caprifoliaceae*) Of the shrubby honeysuckles, two are particularly attractive plants. L. fragrantissima which can grow to thirteen feet and has scented cream-coloured flowers in the dead of winter, and L. nitida Baggesens Gold with golden leaves and an elegant habit of growth.

Some of the best of the climbing honeysuckles are L. americana, L. etrusca superba, and L. japonica Halliana and L. Periclymenum serotina, the late Dutch honeysuckle, and, almost best of all, L. tragophylla, with the largest orange yellow flowers.

Melissa (*Labiatae*) Melissa aurea is a handsome gold leaved form of the ordin-

Jean Jacques Rousseau described carnations as "fit fare for Phoebus' horses" and no flower is more strongly scented

Above Pinks Mrs Sinkins lay a perfumed carpet under a row of old apple trees at Cranborne Manor in Dorset

Left Pinks make neat cushions of silver foliage surmounted by white, crimson-centred flowers with picotee petals

Opposite A terrace with a classic statue as genius loci, and paving stones set with pinks

ary balm and a striking plant for foliage effects.

Mentha (*Labiatae*) The mints not only provide an essential culinary herb but some worthwhile garden plants as well. The decorative variegated mint sometimes has whole stems of pure white leaves, M. Requienii is a prostrate carpeting plant for a damp situation with leaves which give off a pungently pleasant scent when trodden on. M. Pulegium, Pennyroyal, is another quick spreading carpeter with pale purple flowers. There are also mints scented like apple, pineapple, and Eau-de-Cologne, which are all fascinating plants.

Monarda (*Labiatae*) The Bergamots are fine old fashioned border flowers which should be more often planted. Two that are especially attractive are Cambridge Scarlet and the pink, purple-leaved, Beauty of Cobham.

Nicotiana (*Solanaceae*) Tobacco Plants, N. affinis, offer beautiful white flowers

Left *"Lilies would still be beautiful, but sad, if they did not smell" Lilium candidum, the Madonna Lily, and Lilium regale in a cottage setting*
Above *Pale yellow lily Golden Clarion and the tawnier African Queen. Both can grow to a height of five feet*
Opposite *Corner of an Irish garden owned by the distinguished American horticulturist Henry McIlhenny – the towering lilies are the strongly scented Lilium auratum, the star-rayed lily of Japan*

and the most delicious fragrance, their only drawback being that they close their flowers in full sunlight. It is claimed that a new strain, Daylight, does not have this disadvantage. The recently introduced Limegreen, a tobacco with pale green flowers, has great appeal. There are also red nicotianas, but these seem less attractive than the white and green.

Ocimum (*Labiatae*) Basil is a herb which has been cultivated for use in cooking for thousands of years. It is not hardy out of doors in Northern climates, but it is not difficult to grow in a pot. Its leaves are strongly aromatic. Dark Opal is a variant of the ordinary basil, with decorative purple leaves which could be used as a bedding out plant.

Origanum (*Labiatae*) Sweet marjoram, Origanum Majorana, is a plant which is not only useful ground cover, but has bright golden foliage as well.

Philadelphus (*Saxifragaceae*) Five of the best of all the Mock Oranges are

Two garden corners where scented plants "lay their sweetness on the ambient air"

Above *A corner of an Essex garden, in which the aromatic leaves of balm (Melissa officinalis) embower a well placed seat, which in turn, is overcanopied with pale yellow banksian roses (Rosa Banksiae)*

Opposite *A planting scheme of lavender, low growing thymes and roses*

Beauclerc, Belle Etoile (with flowers flushed purple at the centre) coronarius aureus, (with golden leaves) the low growing Manteau d'Hermine, and the strongly scented Sybille.

Rosa (*Rosaceae*) How from the hundreds of roses available to western gardeners can the most captious connoisseur make a choice? And yet, every experienced rose grower or knowledgeable gardener has his or her favourites. The roses recommended on these pages therefore must be accepted as the personal choice of a dedicated rose-lover, who has grown roses for many years, and has written a book on this favourite of all flowers.

Old Shrub Roses Celestial, Queen of Denmark, Louise Odier, Madame Isaac

Pereire, Variegata di Bologna, Chapeau de Napoleon, Fantin Latour, Nuits de Young, William Lobb, Kazanlik, York & Lancaster, Belle de Crécy, Belle Isis, francofurtana (Ex-Imperatrice Josephine) Tuscany Superb. All these old roses, the very pick of the bunch, have been chosen for their beauty of flower, their scent, the harmony between their flowers and foliage and, it must be admitted, for their

romantic evocative associations; for these make a great part of the charm of old roses.

Musk Roses Buff Beauty, Felicia and Penelope.

Rugosa Roses Blanc Double de Coubert, Max Graf (for its odd prostrate growth), Roseraie de L'Haye, Conrad Meyer.

Modern Shrub Roses Aloha, Ballerina, Cerise Bouquet, Clair Matin, Fritz

Above *A brick path hedged with low growing cushiony Santolina Chamaecyparissus, or Cotton lavender, with pungently scented leaves. Above, roses such as Wedding Day and Emily Grey grow through the branches of old apple trees*
Opposite *On a hot day, a herb garden exhales a rich variety of scents. Here lavender, salvia, thyme, fennel and tansy each contribute their special spice*

Nobis, Frühlingsmorgen, Kassel, Margaret Hilling, Nymphenburg, Nevada (with reservations, on account of its ungraceful habit) Raubritter (for its unique shell-like flowers).

Species Roses Persetosa (the enchanting Threepenny Bit rose), filipes Kiftsgate, Hugonis, Moyesii, rubrifolia, Wolley Dod, xanthina Canary Bird, viridiflora (for its odd green flowers – more curious than beautiful).

Floribunda Roses All Gold, Arthur Bell, Beatrice, China Town, City of Belfast, Dearest, Dimples, Elizabeth of Glamis, Galante, Honeymoon, Iceberg, Lavender Lassie, Nypels Perfection, Orangeade, Pernille Poulson, Plentiful Pink Chiffon, Pink Parfait, Rosemary, Santa Maria, Violet Carson.

Hybrid Teas Bond Street, Casanova, Eden Rose, Ena Harkness, Ernest Morse, Grande Mère Jenny, Josephine Bruce, Memoriam, Molly McGredy, Mrs Sam McGredy, Papa Meilland, Shot Silk, Speks Yellow, Superstar, Sutters Gold, Wendy Cussons, Whisky Mac.

Climbing Roses Caroline Testout, Ena Harkness, Peace, Speks Yellow, Cupid, Guinée, Mme Gregoire Staechlin, New Dawn, Pauls Lemon Pillar, Golden

Left *Few shrubs smell so sweetly as the Mock Oranges (philadelphus). One of the best varieties is Belle Etoile – with a purple heart*

Below *Not many rhododendrons are scented – but the Loderi group is an exception, and King George is one of the best. Another late flowering and strongly scented rhododendron is Polar Bear, a cross between R. diaprepes and R. auriculatum*

Opposite *A seat of wrought iron under the flower laden branches of Philadelphus Virginal*

Showers, Parkdirektor Riggers, William Allen Richardson, Amethyste, François Juranville, Wedding Day, Yellow Banksia, sinica Anemone.

Rosemarinus (*Labiatae*) Of the small genus of rosemaries, the most ordinary R. officinalis, is still the best. But two others which are slightly different, and have a charm of their own, are the fastigiate Miss Jessop's Variety, and the miniature, deep blue, Severn Sea.

Tarragon (*Compositae*) There are two kinds of tarragon (Artemisia Dracunculus) French and Russian, and the former is very much the better flavoured

Right "*Most of the buddleias are strongly scented and a great attraction to bees and butterflies*"

Above *A native of Southern Europe, Sweet William, Dianthus barbatus, with its pink, crimson and particoloured flowers has been scenting Western gardens since the 16th century*

Below *A corner of a border in high summer, in which roses and the blue-mauve flowers of Galega officinalis mingle their different scents. In the foreground, the felted flower-spikes of Stachys lanata*

Opposite *Buddleia Davidi Peace has graceful white heads of flowers in late summer*

for cooking, though sometimes difficult to find.

Verbena (*Verbenaceae*) The most effective of all verbenas is surely V. venosa which shows its rich purple flowers for months on end in late summer. In bedding out schemes verbena associates well with geraniums: it is not quite hardy, and in cold gardens its roots should be lifted and stored for the winter.

Above *Eucryphia Nymansay, with white golden-anthered flowers which are delicately scented, and evergreen leaves, is a hybrid of E. cordifolia and E. glutinosa. It will succeed on a chalky soil*
Left *Magnolia stellata originates in Japan and makes a compact shrub, seldom more than five foot high. Its starry flowers have narrow petals. The variety rosea is very pale pink, and rare in cultivation*
Below *Hardy Magnolia Soulangiana Lennei has globe shaped flowers which are white inside and flushed with rosy-purple on the outside*
Opposite *Magnolia Soulangiana alba with flowers as white as pigeons, growing in the shelter of a stone clock tower and soaring cedars of Lebanon at Scotney Castle in Kent*

Above, below and opposite *Lavender and santolina set in squares of brick make a fragrant carpet in a garden in France. Box contributes a subtle smell of its own*
Left *Twin close-clipped plants of helichrysum and lavender make perfumed cushions by steps of brick and stone*
Below left *Helichrysum angustifolium has silver leaves which smell strongly of curry. It delights in poor soil, full sun and sharp drainage*

Groundcover

So much has been written in recent years in books on gardening and in gardening articles on the subject of groundcover, that it is difficult to realize that the very idea of groundcover is quite new. In the days of gardeners (I mean the sort of gardener that Miss Jekyll, rather grandly, refers to as "the resident servant", and not the devoted owner-gardener of today), keeping the ground clear of weeds under shrubs or between herbaceous plants, did not present such a problem. The hoe was constantly at work and as Kipling wrote "Half a proper gardener's work was done upon his knees". But times changed, garden-labour became a most expensive luxury, and fewer gardens had gardeners whose full time job it was to look after them. Or, if they had, there were so many more important tasks to be done, that weeding became a dreaded chore. Then, suddenly, the word groundcover was on everybody's lips. The French (who have in the last few years discovered the pleasure of do-it-yourself gardening) adopted groundcover, making no attempt to translate it, and rolling the "R" in their enthusiasm. Grroundcover joined le five-o'clock, and le footing in the vocabulary of Franglais.

Victoria Sackville-West was one of the first to acclaim the theory of the use of carpeting plants to suppress weeds and dress the bare earth, when in the early fifties, she wrote: "The more I prowl round my garden at this time of year, especially during that stolen hour of dusk between tea and supper, the more do I become convinced that a great secret of good gardening lies in covering every patch of the ground with some suitable carpeter."

But as Miss Sackville-West would have realized better than

Erica makes the most efficient and varied of ground-coverers, as can be seen in this autumnal garden scene. The russet coloured carpet is formed of the late flowering yellow Calluna vulgaris Blazeaway, the green-leaved C. vulgaris alba and pinkish Erica vagans grandiflora. The brilliant red tree in the background is Liquidambar styraciflua, a Sweet Gum from Eastern North America

Anaphalis makes a tight weed-resistant mound of silver foliage surmounted in summer with white immortelle-like flowers

anyone, there are carpeters and carpeters. Sheep and goats. Some are too coarse, some are too invasive (Cerastium tomentosum, Snow-in-Summer, for one, and that over-exuberant Dead Nettle, Lamium Galeobdolon, for another), some do not stand up to heavy shade, and some look poor and thin if planted where the soil is dry.

The ideal groundcovering plant is not one which merely plays the part of another layer of earth, through which weeds can push their way up to the light, and treat the plant as a kind of extra top dressing: plants such as the mossy Arenaria balearica, and the various ground hugging saxifrages, useful though these are.

The ideal groundcoverers - carpeters, weed suppressers, call them what you like - are those that rise a few inches from the surface of the soil like miniature umbrellas, shading the earth beneath and creating an area of darkness which discourages any growth below. Plants which do just this are the invaluable hostas,

and the herbaceous geraniums, especially the excellent Geranium macrorrhizum, which forms a foot-deep blanket of scented leaves and shows attractive pink flowers in spring. Another admirable plant for this purpose is the popular Alchemilla mollis, which has come into such favour during the last few years, with its jade coloured leaves and froth of greenish flowers.

Anaphalis, which makes silver cushions of leaves to the complete discouragement of weeds, is another great ally for the overworked gardener, and the expert Mr Fred Whitsey agrees with me in praising shade-tolerant bergenia, "Evergreen, easy to curb, long flowering in spring - it is a plant of which you can hardly have too much." Mr Whitsey likes to see it planted with tellima, to my mind a rather dull plant. But the round glossy leaves of bergenia go well with so many other kinds of foliage - that of iris especially, or with red leaved plants, such as Rhus cotinus or Perilla frutescens - that it should find a place in every garden.

The low growing polygonums are effective ground-coverers and are crowned with decorative flower for several months on end. P. affine Darjeeling Red is crimson, while the new P. Donald Loundes has red flowers and leaves which colour well in autumn. Both are great spreaders, but easily controlled.

Ajuga (*Labiatae*) The Bugles are all good ground coverers. Ajuga reptans has flowers in spires of blue, white and rose. A. atropurpurea has purple leaves, and A. variegata leaves splashed with white. A. multicolor has foliage flushed with pink.

Alchemilla (*Rosaceae*) Alchemilla mollis is one of the best of all ground coverers with jade green leaves and fluffy heads of greenish flowers which are the delight of flower arrangers.

Anaphalis (*Compositae*) Anaphalis has long lasting silvery leaves and white flowers which can be dried and made into immortelles. A. triplinervis is the variety to choose. Its compact mounds of foliage make excellent ground cover.

Erica (*Ericaceae*) Of the taller ericas, Erica arborea alpina, the Tree Heath is the best and the most hardy. Its foliage is a brighter green than that of the more usually planted E. arborea, and its white flowers are more sweetly scented. A short list of the lower growing heaths, some of the most efficient ground covering plants there are, should certainly include E. carnea (pink flowers and lime tolerant),

Above and **below** *The Erica carnea group is lime tolerant and if planted in bold groups, as here, makes excellent ground cover. E. carnea has pink flowers, and is one of the best. Another good heath of the group is Springwood White. In the picture below, different ericas are shown in effective contrast to a pair of slender upright conifers, Juniperus communis hibernica.*

Opposite *Twin borders in a matching colour scheme of silver and different greens. Some of the plants of which they are composed are the silver and grey leaved santolina, senecio, stachys, artemisia and the acid-green flowers of Alchemilla mollis, a useful ground-coverer, and popular plant for flower-decoration*

E. c. aurea (golden leaved, pink flowered), December Red (flowers in March), and Springwood White. Of the Erica cinereas, Golden Hue, with rich gold leaves and Purple Robe are outstanding, as is the mauve pink Eden Valley. Other good heaths are darleyensis Silver Beads (Silberschmelze), E. tetralix mollis, and E. vagans Holdens Pink, E. v. Lyonesse and E. v. Mrs D. F. Maxwell. It is important, when planting all the smaller heaths, to plant them in groups of at least seven or nine and to work in some peat or leaf-soil around their roots.

Geranium (*Geraniaceae*) The hardy geraniums or Crane's Bills make first class ground cover and some flower throughout the summer. Some of the best are G. armenum with crimson, black centred flowers in July; G. Endressii Major Johnson's Form with larger flowers; macrorrhizum Ingwersens Variety which bears its pink flowers throughout the season, and G. lancastriense with

Above *The front of a border can be kept neat and weed-free by the careful use of mat or cushion forming plants such as the white flowered Iberis sempervirens shown here. The variety Snowflake has larger flower heads than the type*

Below *An effective planting of the silver leaved Stachys lanata, the "ever popular Lambs Lug of cottage gardens" as a close-carpet between round-clipped bushes of yew, Taxus baccata*

Opposite above *Thick spreading plants of differing foliage make a leafy weed-free balustrade for a flight of brick steps. On one side are the low clinging branches of Cotoneaster horizontalis – on the other the handsome leaves of Vitis Coignetiae, a vine which colours well in autumn*

Below left and right *The shrubby salvias make effective weed smotherers if clipped every spring to encourage thicker, wider growth. To the left – Purple leaved Salvia officinalis atropurpurea, to the right S. officinalis aurea, with golden leaves. S. tricolor – the Painted Sage, with leaves edged with white, and tinged with pink, is a real plant for the connoisseur*

attractive silky leaves and flesh coloured flowers.

Lamium (*Labiatae*) The Dead-nettles are all great weed suppressors – though L. Galeobdolon, which has silver variegated leaves, is almost too rampant for most gardens. More restrained are L. maculatum with mauve or pale pink flowers – or L. maculatum aureum, an attractive slower growing form, with pale gold leaves.

Polygonum (*Polygonaceae*) There are two excellent low growing polygonums. P. affine Darjeeling Red which has miniature spikes of crimson flowers, and the new Donald Loundes, with red flowers and foliage which colours well in autumn.

Stachys (*Labiatae*) Stachys lanata is the ever popular Lamb's Lug of cottage gardens, with leaves like silver velvet. Stachys macrantha superba is an excellent plant with dark green hirsute foliage and handsome mauve heads of flowers. Both are great ground coverers.

Above *A shady path of classic paving stones is bordered on one side by a carpet of wild garlic, Allium triquetrum, an odoriferous and rampantly spreading onion, best kept to the wilder parts of the garden, though it is an efficient carpeter for a shady site.*

Below *"The hardy geraniums or Crane's-bills make first class groundcover and some flower throughout the summer". Geranium armenum has crimson, black centred flowers and makes a handsome mound of leaf and flower in high summer*

Opposite above *A bank completely blanketed in different greens, with Juniperus communis hibernica as exclamation mark, and Erica tetralix williamsiana and Erica cinerea atrorubens to keep all weeds in check*

Below *On top of a wall in the well drained soil it most appreciates, Santolina Chamaecyparissus, the Cotton Lavender, makes tight cushions of aromatic silver leaves if clipped well back in spring. Below Hostas, especially the bold Hosta glauca, with its blue-green spreading leaves make very effective groundcoverers*

Above *The white-piped leaves of Hosta crispula effectively cover the ground at the angle of a wall. Its flowers, borne on graceful stems, are pale violet*

Above right *Alchemilla mollis, or colloquially, Lady's Mantle, covers the ground with its umbrella shaped jade green leaves and fluffy flower heads of acid green. Alchemilla delights in a cool position and is a generous seeder in a limey soil*

Below *Beyond a mat of stachys, Lamium maculatum lays a chequered carpet. Dead nettles are excellent weed suppressors and quick spreaders. Lamium maculatum aureum has luminous pale yellow leaves, but is of more restrained growth. Its flowers are mauve*

Opposite *Good border planning should include groups of plants of different form and leaf to give contrast – with low growing clumps in the front to make a definite, if informal, outline. Here Stachys lanata – blue flowered Nepeta Mussinii (of which Six Hills Giant is the most imposing form) and Sedum spectabile edge a herbaceous border in the traditional style*

Below left *To edge a hot dry path there are few brighter, more spreading plants than Mesembryanthemum criniflorum*

Below right *Campanula carpatica lays a blue swathe below the large leaves of Yucca filamentosa*

Above *Bergenia cordifolia, close planted at the base of a Japanese lantern in a Hampshire garden. All the bergenias are good ground coverers, with their glossy evergreen leaves and spreading habit. B. cordifolia has rosy pink flowers in early spring, B. crassifolia has particularly handsome crinkled leaves, and the Ballawley Hybrids the largest crimson flower heads*

Below *Cushions of santolina surround the base of standard Buddleia Peace, in an originally planned Essex garden*

Opposite *Evergreen and ever-grey plants, such as box, santolina, and senecio, make a tapestry of muted colours (and a planting scheme needing little upkeep) at Eydon Hall near Rugby*

Walls

Gardens of today are smaller than the gardens of the past, and every available planting space must be utilized. Gardening must be vertical as well as horizontal. Walls offer an ideal opportunity for growing the most fascinating plants, which at ground level take up but little space - a square foot at most - but can spread their leaves and flowers over a large area at eye level or higher. Unsightly fences can be made to flower like borders - new brick walls can be veiled with green.

But a word of warning - from a gardener of half a century ago, Miss Gertrude Jekyll - "Where there is beautiful architectural proportion . . . it is obvious that it would be most unwise to let it be over-run with creepers", and Miss Jekyll goes on to advise "watchful restraint", and then careful choice, of such climbing plants which set off the building, without smothering it entirely.

Few gardeners today have house walls of old Tudor brick - or of the purest classical proportions, such as one finds in old Colonial houses. But there are still houses in America and Europe which look better unadorned, even with vines or roses.

It is a case of the gardener versus the architect: Miss Jekyll goes on - "The horticulturist generally errs in putting his plants and shrubs and climbers everywhere . . . the architect, on the other hand, is often wanting in sympathy for vegetation." It is a question of give and take. As a general rule, ivy is not a desirable wall-coverer - unless the wall is really an eye-sore. On house walls, ivy harbours birds and insects, and makes unwelcome inroads into the brickwork and drainpipes. That great expert on gardens, the late Christopher Hussey, inveighed against ivy on old buildings - describing it as a "worthless and sentimental smudge," and corners covered with ivy as "vaguely old-fashioned, in a stuffy and fustian way." But the ivy he so disliked was ordinary ivy. The ivies listed in this chapter are ivies, none of

Above *Classic covering for walls are climbing roses. Here the old favourite Crimson Conquest grows surprisingly happily in an old lead container*
Opposite *Clematis, ideal plants for walls or fences, prefer to have their roots in shade, their flowers in full sun. The large-flowered varieties are particularly decorative, such as the white Marie Boisselot shown here. Another good white clematis, with a darker centre, is henryi*

which are very rare, but which are plants of distinction and of less rampant growth than the type. Vitis baldschuanicum - the Russian Vine - is unlovely except in very hot summers, when it can put on a fine show of white frothing flowers, but is useful as a quick climber. Though the connoisseur may sniff at ampelopsis, both the useful self-clinging Virginia Creepers (A. quinquefolia and A. veitchii) have their uses, and they can look beautiful in autumn. Vitis Henryana has particularly delicately coloured foliage.

But there are many other, more desirable climbing plants. Wisteria is perhaps the best of all - for it enhances old brick or stonework but does not obliterate it. The curious multi-coloured leaved actinidia is a wall shrub that can easily be kept within bounds. Many roses, most vines, especially Vitis atropurpurea, which is a more special plant than the popular V. Coignetiae, embellish walls. And the climbing potato, Solanum crispum, is a climber that might be planted more often.

And then there are the shrubs which can be effectively grown on walls, because the added protection enables them to flourish as they would never do in the open. Many of these "wall shrubs" would grow perfectly happily, free standing, in climates benigner than those of North America and Britain, but due to the rigours of Northern winters and springs, they benefit immensely from some protection, and so have come to be given positions sheltered by a wall. A short list would certainly include ceanothus, choisya, and the incomparable camellia.

But whatever shrubs and climbers are chosen to dress a garden wall, they should be chosen with care. Walls should never be totally hidden by too exuberant vegetation. The eyes, even of gardeners who should know better, to quote Christopher Hussey once more "grow accustomed . . . and fail to notice the growth of the stuff. Owing, no doubt, to their preoccupation with more intellectual matters, the authorities of Oxford and Cambridge Colleges are particularly prone to this form of myopia."

Left *Happiest growing in the shelter of a wall, in sharply drained soil is the late summer flowering Perovskia atriplicifolia, with blue flowers, and feathery silver foliage*
Opposite *Honeysuckle curtaining a wall* *by a gate in a Chinese Chippendale design. Three of the best are Lonicera belgica – Early Dutch, with red and yellow flowers, the almost evergreen L. Halliana, and L. serotina, Late Dutch, which flowers in July on to October*

Above *Humulus scandens aureus, the Golden Hop, shows brilliant yellow leaves in early summer and can quickly top a fifteen foot wall. It is useful for making a quick, and decorative, screen*

Left *Vitis Henryana is the best of all Virginia Creepers, with more refined leaves than the type, darker green, more elegantly veined, and colouring well in autumn*

Opposite above *The most effective of all ivies is Hedera canariensis Gloire de Marengo, with its large leaves, dappled in white and green*

Below *Actinidia Kolomikta, unlike its relation Actinidia chinensis, is of "the mildest disposition", slow growing but well worth waiting for, on account of its uniquely showy leaves with their odd splashings of white and pink*

Actinidia (*Actinidiaceae*) Two actinidias are well worth garden space, but they need very different positions. Actinidia chinensis has to be placed with great care, because, though extremely handsome, it is a rampant climber, and can pull down small trees with its long hairy arms. Actinidia Kolomikta, on the other hand, is of the mildest disposition, and seldom reaches a height of more than eight feet. If planted on a south wall, the three-coloured variegation (white, rose and green) of its leaves, which is the beauty of the plant, will be more developed.

Aristolochia (*Aristolochiaceae*) Climbers with beautiful fern-like foliage, and flowers which are pipe-shaped and a brilliant orange. For warmer districts only. A. Sipho is the variety to look for.

Caesalpinia (*Leguminoseae*) C. alpina is a real shrub for the connoisseur, though it needs a mild climate and a sheltered position on a wall. Its canary-yellow flowers with bright red stamens, present the most exotic picture.

Camellia (*Theaceae*) Camellias are far hardier than was once supposed, and will tolerate some lime in the soil, though they prefer this to be acid. Chief threat to camellias is early morning sunshine on the leaves after frost, so a west or north facing wall suits them best. Out of the hundreds of species and hybrid camellias listed, here are some which are of proven worth – Camellia reticulata, perhaps the best of all, C. saluenensis, C. Sasanqua, C. Williamsii (saluenensis X japonica), especially the hybrids Donation and J. C. Williams. Of the innumerable hybrids of C. japonica, Adolphe Audusson (blood red), Comtesse Lavinia Maggi (striped white and cerise), chandleri elegans (pink flaked with white), the rose pink, long flowering Gloire de Nantes, Lady Clare (semi-double, pink), and pure white mathotiana alba, are all first class plants.

Campsis (*Bignoniaceae*) These are showy climbers for a sheltered wall, with pinnate leaves and pendant orange trumpet flowers. C. chinensis, Madame Galen, is hardier than most.

Carpenteria (*Saxifragaceae*) Carpenterias are handsome white flowered

shrubs to grow against a wall; but they are apt to be short lived. The best form to plant is Ladham's Variety; once planted, it should never be disturbed.

Ceanothus (*Rhamnaceae*) For blue flowering shrubs ceanothus take the prize. They are lime tolerant and good plants for seaside gardens. Six of the very best are the evergreen Autumnal Blue, and the rich blue Delight, the dark blue densely-growing dentatus, thyrsiflorus and the unusual rosy pink Perle Rose. Topaz is a richer blue than the commoner, summer-flowering Gloire de Versailles.

Choisya (*Rutaceae*) Choisya ternata, The Mexican Orange Blossom, is a most attractive evergreen shrub with spicy leaves and cream-white flowers. It is only really happy against a wall.

Cistus (*Cistaceae*) Cistus delight in poor soil and full sun. They thrive on chalk, but resent disturbance. C. corbariensis is perhaps the hardiest: it has white flowers and fresh green leaves. C. cyprius, with white flowers marked with crimson, can grow to a height of nine feet. C. pulverulentus (Sunset) is one of the most attractive of all cistus, with silvery leaves and pink flowers, as has the most beautiful hybrid Silver Pink. C. algarvensis makes a neat low shrub covered with yellow flowers. All the last three are good plants for paving.

Clematis (*Ranunculaceae*) The large flowered clematis are among the most beautiful of climbers – and they thrive with their flowers in the sun, and their roots in the shade. The north side of a low wall facing south, is their ideal position. Out of the hundreds available, a

Above *Wisteria drapes a wall as effectively as any other climber, and its mauve, sharply scented flowers are in full beauty in early summer. Wisteria floribunda macrobotrys (multijuga) has particularly long and graceful racemes*

Below *Clematis montana is one of the most generous of spring flowerers and will quickly curtain any wall. In the background and appreciative of its sheltered position, Ceanothus impressus*

list of a few very special plants might include Belle of Woking, with silvery mauve flowers that are sometimes almost green, the rose-coloured Comtesse de Bouchard, the wine-red Ernest Markham, deep purple Victoria, semi-herbaceous Durandii, cream white Henryi, sun-loving white Huldine, white Madame Boisselot, favourite Lasurstern, pale blue Mrs Cholmondely, and deep purple The President.

Species or smaller flowered clematis have their own fascination, and are sometimes easier to grow than the showier hybrids. All very desirable plants are the Francis Rivis form of C. alpina, C. Armandii and C. chrysocoma. The winter flowering C. calycina, the pink forms of C. montana, Pink Perfection or rubens, C. Rehderiana with flowers of pale primrose in autmn – the yellow C. tangutica, not only for its flowers but for its feathery seed pods, too: and the rare C. texensis with small vase-shaped scarlet flowers, and the pink flowered, vigorous C. vedrariensis rosea. For the border there are several attractive herbaceous clematis. C. heracleifolia Campanile, with rich mauve hyacinth flowers, being one of the best.

Clianthus (*Leguminosae*) The Lobster Claw plant has the most exotic appearance but will only succeed, in the open

Above Magnolias, jasmines and vines revel in the warmth of the walls of a balustraded terrace at historic Powis Castle, in Wales. In front are box-bordered beds of sweet smelling heliotrope and standard fuchsias

Below An elegant hydrangea which is at its best against a wall is the velvety leaved Hydrangea Sargentiana, which can grow eight foot high, and shows white flowers on slightly bristled stems. Next to it grows a real plant for the connoisseur, Ozothamnus rosmarinifolium, from Tasmania, with dark green leaves and showy pink buds which open into pale cream flowers. Ozothamnus, also known as Helichrysum rosmarinifolium, is a shrub for a mild climate, and needs wall protection even then

air, in the most sheltered position and in sharply drained soil. Its flowers are bright red. There is a less arresting, but rarer, white form – Clianthus puniceus albus.

Cobaea Scandens (*Polemoniaceae*) One of the fastest of all climbers – cobaea is not hardy in Northern gardens, but can be readily raised from seed and planted out, when it will shoot up to a height of eight or nine feet in no time. Its bells are greenish-purple, and will last well if cut. The white form is less attractive.

Convolvulus (*Convolvulaceae*) Of the many convolvulus there are three which are well worth growing. The low shrubby C. Cneorum – with grey leaves and white flowers flushed with pink, and two annual

convolvulus, the well known blue C. major (Morning Glory) and C. minor Crimson Monarch.

Cotoneaster (*Rosaceae*) Cotoneasters are the most easy going of shrubs and will succeed in almost any soil or situation. Some are prostrate in form – others make elegant trees; most berry and colour brightly in autumn.

A few for the connoisseur are C. aldenhamensis, C. bullata macrophylla, C. conspicua decora, with particularly bright berries, the ground-hugging C. Dammeri, the brilliantly autumn colouring C. disticha tongolensis; the variegated form of the popular C. horizontalis, and the easily trained hybridus pendulus.

Crinum (*Amaryllidaceae*) The Cape

Above *Clematis montana, whether in its usual white form or the less common Clematis montana Pink Perfection is one of the glories of early summer. Clematis montana is so robust that it has been described as the ideal covering for "Twentieth century eye-sores – such as garages."*
Right *Clematis Fair Rosamond with striking purple stamened centres*
Opposite above *Clematis Durandii has a semi-herbaceous habit and is ideal to grow through other shrubs, as here, where it drapes a dense plantation of erica*
Centre *The popular Clematis Jackmannii catches the evening sun on the angle of a wall*
Below *One of the best of all clematis in late summer is the rosy purple Victoria*

Lilies are handsome late summer flowering plants for a warm position and in well drained soil, such as the foot of a wall. C. Powellii has rose pink trumpet flowers. C. p. album is white. C. p. Krelagei has extra large pale rose flowers.

Cydonia (*Rosaceae*) Chaenomeles is the beloved "japonica" of one's childhood, and has suffered several changes of name in the last twenty years, having been known as Pyrus japonica, chaenomeles, and cydonia. The best of the flowering quinces are C. lagenaria Brilliant (Bright red), nivalis (white), and the best of all, Knaphill Scarlet. C. moerloesii has flowers like apple-blossom.

Desmodium (*Leguminoseae*) This is a plant which came to Europe in the year of Queen Victoria's accession. Its arching branches, weighed down with mauve pea flowers in late summer, make it the ideal plant for the top of a hot bank, or low wall. Also known as lespedeza.

Eccremocarpus (*Bignoniaceae*) Eccremocarpus scaber is a showy climbing plant for a warm south wall, covered with a mass of tubular·orange flowers in

late summer. It should be raised from seed and planted out in May.

Fremontia (*Sterculiaceae*) The quick growing Fremontia californica is a true plant for the connoisseur, but needs the warmest and most sheltered position against a wall. Its large yellow flowers are borne from early summer until October.

Hedera (*Araliaceae*) There are several ivies of great distinction, Hedera colchica variegata is the best of all large leaved golden ivies. H. Helix Cavendishii has silvery leaves, but is a slow grower. H. cristata has unusual fringed leaves, while H. tricolor has leaves edged with white

Opposite *Wisteria curtains the corner of an old English manor in Sussex*

Above *Choisya ternata, the Mexican Orange Blossom, only gives of its best in the shelter of a wall. Its flowers are creamy-white, and its dark green leaves are spicily scented*

Above right *Roses wreath the walls and terrace of a Georgian house in Gloucestershire. Rose on the grey stone wall of the house is the copper budded Albertine, a hybrid wichuriana*

Right *A climber for the connoisseur, equally happy draping an evergreen, as here, or a shaded wall. In either position it likes a cool moist root run, and peat worked into the soil when planted: Tropaeolum speciosum*

and pink. H. Buttercup is a rich yellow.

Helichrysum (*Compositae*) Two helichrysums that are well worth growing are the strongly aromatic Curry Plant, H. serotinum, and the more delicate rosmarinifolium (also known as Ozothamnus rosmarinifolius) with showy pink bead-like buds opening to creamy flowers. This needs the protection of a wall in northern gardens.

Jasminum (*Oleaceae*) Five desirable jasmines, other than the indispensable J. nudiflorum and J. officinale, are the larger stronger-growing officinale grandiflorum, and J. revolutum, which make elegant semi-evergreen shrubs with large yellow flowers: the delicate Primrose jasmine – J. primulinum with yellow flowers and the strongly scented J. polyanthum which needs greenhouse protection in all but the mildest districts. The hybrid jasmine – J. stephanense – pink flowers and of rampant growth is also worth growing.

Othonnopsis (*Compositae*) Othonnopsis cheirifolia is not often grown, but it is a most useful plant, with glaucous strap-shaped leaves which can most effectively drape a low wall or bank – but it is its leaves and unusual habit, which are the charm of othonnopsis.

Passiflora (*Passifloraceae*) Passiflora caerulea is one of the most beautiful and evocative plants to be grown – and the white form, Constance Elliott, is equally fine. Hardier, however, than both of

Left *Callistemon salignus from Australia, needs the shelter of a wall in all but the mildest climates. Its bottle-brush shaped flowers are remarkable for their bright yellow whiskery stamens*

Below *Euonymus radicans variegatus is a silver and gold, small leaved shrub which loves to climb a wall, though it takes a long time to reach the height of the one illustrated here. It will also make excellent groundcover*

Opposite *Honeysuckle and rosemary under the old red brick walls of Sissinghurst Castle in Kent, where there is one of the most beautiful gardens in the world*

Above *Spiraea arguta. The Bridal Wreath bush will quickly grow to a height of eight or ten feet if given wall protection. Grown in this way, it is one of the airiest and freshest of all wall coverers*

Opposite *Banksian roses shower a sun-baked wall in an Italian garden. Rosa Banksiae, one of the most poetic and classic of all roses, needs a sheltered site and the lightest pruning. It was named after Lady Banks, wife of Sir Joseph Banks, the great botanist*

Below left *A plant which needs wall protection and hot sun is the Coral Tree, Erythrina Crista-galli, while for a shady wall, there are few more rewarding plants than fuchsias* **right** *which will thrive away from direct sunshine and in a cool position*

these, is P. umbilicata, with attractive small violet flowers.

Phygelius (*Scrophulariaceae*) The Cape Figwort, if given the protection of a wall in northern gardens, will grow to a height of eight to ten feet and show its scarlet flowers from June until the first frosts. It also makes a useful border plant. P. capensis coccineus is the best variety.

Piptanthus (*Leguminosae*) Piptanthus, from Nepal, grows well in any well drained soil and is tolerant of chalk. Its yellow pea flowers show up well when the shrub is planted against a wall. P. nepalensis is the one to choose.

Sisyrinchium (*Iridaceae*) The Satin Flowers or Rush Lilies make attractive plants to grow in paving where their Iris-like foliage makes elegant tufts, contrasting well with stone work. They are generous seeders.

Solanum (*Solanaceae*) The best of all the decorative climbing potatoes is the chalk-loving, long flowering Glasnevin form of Solanum crispum.

Tropaeolum (*Tropaeolaceae*) Two distinguished nasturtiums are T. peregrinum, the Canary Creeper, with trailing fronds of glaucous leaves and masses of yellow flowers in June. It is a half hardy perennial: and T. speciosum which, once it is established, will drape rhododendrons or other shrubs, with festoons of scarlet flowers year after year. It likes damp soil, and some peat.

Valerian (*Valerianaceae*) Valerian (Ken-

tranthus) naturalizes easily in walls. The rosy-carmine and white forms (K. macrosiphon) are more desirable plants than the more usual red. Valerian is a great seeder.

Vitis (*Vitaceae*) Of the many ornamental vines six are outstanding. V. Davidi cyanacarpa with particularly luxuriant leaves which colour well in autumn: V. vinifera Brant which fruits well in Northern gardens, and its purple leaved form, purpurea; V. fragola with strawberry-flavoured fruit; V. Henryana (Parthenocissus Henryana), by far the most refined of the Virginia Creepers, self clinging with leaves that are veined in pink and white. And a most effective vine for any gardener, connoisseur or not, is still the ever popular V. Coignetiae, especially in its purple-leaved form.

Wisteria (*Leguminoseae*) The best of all wisterias is W. floribunda macrobotrys (multijuga) of which the falling racemes can be 3 feet long or more. Two more unusual wisterias are the white W. venusta and the almost pink W. floribunda rosea.

Above *Othonnopsis cheirifolia "is not often grown, but is a most useful plant with glaucous strap-shaped leaves". It delights in a position where it can grow downward over a wall or a steep bank. Its yellow daisy flowers are borne over a long period*
Below *The almost vertical face of a dry wall is the position in which to plant sempervivum or House Leek – said to ward off evil spirits. Grown in this way they display their rosettes effectively, and will quickly make large clumps, needing only the minimum of moisture. To the right, a silver tuft of the Sheep's Fescue, Festuca glauca, a miniature grass which seldom grows more than nine inches high*
Opposite *Carpenteria californica is one of the loveliest shrubs which Europe owes to America (it was introduced in 1880). It prefers the shelter of a wall and shows its many anthered, sweet smelling flowers in June. Carpenteria was named after the distinguished American botanist William Carpenter (1811–1848) of Louisiana*

Paving

There are many plants, besides weeds, which delight in growing in paving. Some make attractive cushions of flower and verdure, while there are others which grow in low, ground-hugging mats, and seem not to resent the occasional foot-fall, but, masochistically to thrive on, or rather under, it. Such plants add immensely to the beauty of a paved terrace, or path of informally set stones.

The flower beneath the foot is no new idea - no special carpet laid for Firbank's sad heroine, in his novel of that name. In the 16th century, Francis Bacon advised gardeners to set paths of scented, low-growing herbs, "to have the pleasure when you walk or tread". Today a terrace is a highly valued feature of a garden, especially of small houses; for in summer a terrace offers extra living space, and in wet weather affords a part of the garden which can be visited dry shod.

In a garden in Long Island the author remembers a terrace of old grey stone of which the interstices had been planted with peppermint - which scented the air deliciously, especially when trodden on after rain. And in Essex, he knows a sundial around the base of which (the area that Humpty Dumpty in "Through the looking glass" would have called the Wabe "because it goes a long way before it, and a long way behind it") had been set with thyme, both gold and silver varieties; an excusable horticultural pun.

There are many plants which lend themselves ideally to such a position though thyme is perhaps the ideal one. Acaena, a seldom grown plant from New Zealand, is a perfect plant for paving. It has jade green filigree leaves - which are covered in late summer with pink hedgehog-burrs which attach themselves to trouser cuffs, and seed themselves about. Mentha Pulegium (Pennyroyal) is another creeper, especially over damp stones, which brightens the ground with its largesse of golden pennies. This, like thyme, gives off a faint and evocative fragrance when

Above *Thymus Serpyllum coccineum lays a purple carpet. To the right, Doryncnium hirsutum, with white flowers*
Opposite *In a Scottish garden Phlox subulata Temiscaming laps a terrace made of old Edinburgh street paving stones. Beyond the rock, Viola gracilis major*

Lavender, pinks and mat-forming plants in a paved corner of the great Yorkshire garden at Newby Hall

walked on. Two hundred years ago its leaves were used by the very poor as a substitute for tea. Pennyroyal is a mint, and another mint, Mentha Requieni, is one of the best of all creeping plants to cover cool stonework. It exhales a delicious peppermint smell. Arenaria balearica is another creeping moss-like plant for paving, starred in summer with tiny white flowers. The pink-flowered Erinus alpinus is another charming plant for paving. Many of the alpine phlox, such as the robust subulata, nivalis and pale blue divarica, are first class plants for paving: though why they are described as alpine is a mystery: almost all originate in America. A plant often grown and very much to be avoided is the dread Snow-in-Summer, Cerastium tomentosum. This is a

rampageous spreader - not that rampageousness is a bad quality, when the ever exuberant plant in question allows itself to be pulled up in one piece and thrown away. But cerastium does not, and once established it is almost impossible to eradicate, especially when its roots run under stone.

Though this book deals primarily with plants, two pieces of advice to would-be pavement gardeners might not be out of place here. First, it is best for all paving to be discreetly pointed, that is, to have the joints cemented firmly, leaving fissures between the stones at least an inch deep, but no more. This will allow mosses to grow but no deep rooting weeds; and second: spaces that are left for "paving" plants should be filled with really good soil.

Low growing golden-flowered Hypericum olympicum, and deep purple dwarf lavender make comfortable cushions of flower on a south-facing terrace

Acaena (*Rosaceae*) The New Zealand Burr is a fascinating plant with grey and bronze ferny foliage and bright crimson seed heads in late summer. It is excellent to grow in paving, and seeds itself generously.

Alyssum (*Cruciferae*) For dry walls or for growing in paving, few plants are brighter than the Madworts. A. saxatile citrinum with pale lemon flowers is kinder to the eye than the loud A. saxatile. Dudley Neville is a subtle biscuit colour, and the best of the lot.

Arenaria (*Caryophyllaceae*) Arenaria is an excellent moss forming plant to clothe cool stonework or the base of walls. A. balearica has tiny white starry flowers, and grows well in shade. A. purpurascens, with pinkish flowers, prefers full sun.

Campanula (*Campanulaceae*) Of the taller campanulas – C. lactiflora Loddon Anna (lilac), C. persicifolia alba (white), C. perisicifolia Telham Beauty (single blue), and Pouffe, a lower growing cushiony variety, with cup shaped mauve flowers are the best. Of the innumerable smaller varieties C. carpatica Blue Moon-Light, C. carpatica White Star, C. muralis major, C. pilosa superba, flowering in May, and C. warleyensis, flowering in August, are all good plants for paving or rock work.

Dianthus (*Caryophyllaceae*) Carnations or dianthus take their name from the Greek; Dios, a God, and anthos, a flower, and there are few of the genus which do not live up to their name. Though there is no place in this book for the green-

Above left *Silver leaved plants such as the airy Artemisia Palmeri, helichrysum, and different thymes border a stone-edged path. Between the paving stones, Chrysanthemum poterium, which makes flat cushions of tiny feathery tufts of leaves, that are nearly pure white*

Left and **opposite** *Cerastium tomentosum, "Snow-in-Summer" makes an effective plant in paving, but can be too invasive, and once planted, is difficult to eradicate. C. tomentosum Columnae is a neater, less rampant grower*

house varieties of carnation, such as the marvellously opulent Malmaisons, there are several rock garden and border varieties which well deserve a mention. The mat-forming pink-flowered Dianthus arvernensis, erinaceus and La Bourbrille, are all attractive plants for paving, or for gritty pockets in the rock garden. D. deltoides Steriker has flowers which are a rich crimson.

For the border there are several fascinating hybrids such as the chocolate flowered French Lace, the raspberry coloured Jonathan and the pale mauve Lavender Lady. Best of all, and taking the place in the garden once held by Mrs Sinkins, is the pure white, strongly fragrant Swan Lake.

Allwood is a famous name in the carnation world, and one of the most attractive of all pinks was raised by Montagu Allwood. It is called Loveliness and its unique shredded petals give it an airy lacy quality all of its own.

Schizostylis (*Iridaceae*) The finest of the Kaffir Lilies, S. coccinea grandiflora, is Mrs Hegarty, with rose coloured flowers in October. Schizostylis need a warm position at the foot of a wall, and some protection in winter. It makes a fine exclamation mark if grown in paving.

Sempervivum (*Crassulaceae*) All the houseleeks have fascinating leaves, and make tight clusters in rock work or on the top of walls. They are said to ward off evil spirits. The cobweb houseleek – S. arachnoideum – has cobwebby rosettes of leaves and deep pink flowers. Granat has particularly neat dark red foliage.

Above *Informal paving set about with pots of petunias and tufts of dianthus and iris*
Below *Old fashioned flowers, such as pinks and candytuft, Iberis amara, stud a lavender bordered terrace in Ireland. Candytuft Tom Thumb in an improved, more compact form*
Opposite *Some plants associate particularly happily with paving – such as all the valerians, Valeriana officinalis, either in its white, pink or crimson form*

Thymus (*Labiatae*) There are several thymes which have a very special charm. The golden lemon-scented citriodorus aureus, and its silver leaved form Silver Queen. T. nitidus makes a compact grey foliaged shrublet. There are three enchanting forms of the creeping T. Serpyllum – the pink Annie Hall, crimson coccineus, and rosy pink Chintz.

Above *In early spring – the pink flowers of Bergenia crassifolia, here growing in brickwork, show before the large, green leaves appear*

Above left *The Satin Iris, Sisyrinchium striatum, not only delights to grow in paving, and readily seeds itself about, but will thrive in gravel, too. Its flowers are pale yellow, with a darker eye*

Left *Sedum spathulifolium with mauve, frosted leaves, grows happily in the back of an old stone seat. Its flowers are yellow, and borne in high summer*

Opposite above *Lavender and mat-forming thymes and sedums clothe a low flight of stone steps*

Below *A terrace which is almost too overgrown. To be effective, pavement planting should always be kept in strict control*

Shade

In the days of larger gardens - and more gardeners - shade tolerant plants were not so important as they are today. In country gardens, areas under trees, or on the north side of walls, were just kept tidy, but seldom made much of. Gardeners concentrated on the parts of their gardens where growing conditions were more favourable; and shaded areas were lucky if they were planted with periwinkle or ground ivy. Dark corners of country gardens still tend to be treated in this way.

The growing interest in city gardening has changed things, and even in country gardens (especially if they are quite small) gardeners have grown to feel that every bit of space must be made the most of. In town gardens, of course, shade-tolerant plants really come into their own, and have an all important role to play. Books and innumerable magazine articles, have been written on plants which will put up with the disadvantages of city life.

City gardeners have learned much in the last thirty years. First, they have learned how rewarding a town garden, however small, can be. Formerly town gardens were the domain of the dog or cat, and usually dank, dark and neglected. Laurels were their dingy pride. Second, town gardeners have learned that only certain plants thrive under city conditions. They must know what to plant. Third, they have learned that thorough soil preparation is advisable, and that drainage must be checked. Fourth, and almost the most important, constant watering is essential.

The drawback in almost every city is lack of direct sunshine. Though a tree in a town garden is a godsend, it can exclude much needed light, as well as impoverish the soil. Plants for city use, except in exceptional circumstances, must therefore be strong growing and tolerant of shade.

It took the author of this book years to appreciate, for instance the charm of hostas. They seemed to him to be gloomy plants, good only to plant where nothing else would grow. And it is true

Above *All fuchsias are happiest out of direct sunshine. F. versicolor has attractive foliage, flecked with gold, to set off its many pendant flowers*
Opposite *The Tibetan blue poppies are among the most beautiful of all plants to grow in shade – but need lime-free soil, a moist, but well drained situation, and a rich diet of peat or leaf-mould. Shown here is Meconopsis grandis, of which Branklyn is one of the best forms*

that until recently, hostas were often planted not only in the shade, but also in dry, arid spots where no plant could be expected to give of its best. For the soil in shady places, though cool, can also be as dry as dust. Now all that has changed, and gardeners have come to realize that, to show their leaves in their fullest beauty - and with hostas, their leaves are the thing - hostas must not only grow in shade, but in rich, moist soil as well.

Some special attention has been given to hostas - until recently known as funkias - though why the Austrian Doktor Nickolaus Host has a better claim to be commemorated by such a good plant, than the German apothecary Heinrich Funk, has never been made clear. Hostas deserve this special attention as they are the shade plant *par excellence*. And the rule which goes for them - that they will grow in shade, but must have reasonably acceptable growing conditions - goes for all shade plants, fuchsias, acanthus, Solomons Seal or that dreary, but long

suffering plant, so popular for some reason in America, pachy-sandra. They will only give of their best if the soil in which they are to be planted is well prepared, enriched with fertilizer, and, above all, kept moist.

Even ferns, which are so beautiful in shaded gardens (the Victorians, who loved ferns, called them "vegetable jewellery") need well prepared soil and a lacing of peat before they will show off their filigree leaves to the best advantage.

So, if gardeners want their shade to be green, let them give a green thought to it. Then, as a talented gardener of the last century, Shirley Hibbert, once wrote: "If the basic needs of plants that are required to grow in such disadvantageous places are considered, the plants' goodwill should receive its just deserts. If this is done, they will surely respond, and repay the owner of the darkest and most sunless garden with flowers as good as they can give, and with refreshing verdure for much of the year."

Above *A magnolia, feathery leaved Artemisia arborescens, and a yucca in full flower set a varied garden scene at a street corner in Kensington*

Opposite above *In a leafy corner, the white flowers of petunia are unscorched by sun, while behind, flourish the luxuriant foliage of Althaea rosea. To the right, shade-tolerant Mahonia lomariifolia, named for the American botanist Bernard M'Mahon (1775–1816)*

Below *Ferns, ivies and the round-leaved Bergenia cordifolia are three faithful stand-bys for would-be city gardeners*

Aconitum (*Ranunculaceae*) The monks-hoods offer flowers in several colours. The purple Aconitum Delavayi, the favourite blue (or white) Napellus, and the good new pale blue Sparkes Variety. A real plant for gardeners looking for something unusual is the climbing acon-ite, A. volubile which will grow up to eight feet on a wall or pillar.

Above *An exotic looking plant with handsome leaves, which will thrive in deepest shade is Fatsia japonica, a real friend for town gardeners. Its flowers are ivory-coloured and borne in bracts*
Above left *Acanthus grows well in partial shade, whether A. mollis is chosen, or A. spinosus, with more deeply toothed leaves. Acanthus leaves have been the inspiration of architects down the centuries. A less classic, but descriptive, name for the plant is Bear's Breeches. To the left – the ever useful hosta, and to the right, a yucca*
Below *Ivies are hardworking plants for shady town gardens, and the golden leafed variety, Hedera helix Buttercup will brighten up any dark corner*
Opposite *Ivies, Virginia Creeper, jasmine and the opulent leaves of hydrangeas clothe in green, a shaded Chelsea garden*

Aquilegia (*Ranunculaceae*) The columbines are excellent plants for town gardens – their foliage persisting in beauty long after the flowers are past. Two for the discerning gardener are the red and white Crimson Star, and the new McKana hybrids, with large flowers in mixed colours. A. Skinneri is a rare species aquilegia from Guatamala, with yellow and orange flowers.

Arundinaria (*Gramineae*) Bamboos grow well in town gardens, and in country ones they are useful as screens or by the waterside. Arundinaria falcata (syn Bambusa gracilis) A. Murielae and A. nitida, are three of the best to choose.

Bergenia (*Saxifragaceae*) Bergenia, or Saxifraga megasea, will grow almost anywhere, in shade, in tubs, and looks well planted in the front of shrub borders. They thrive in city gardens.

B. cordifolia and B. cordifolia purpurea are both good plants while the Ballawley hybrids are a great improvement on the form. For foliage fans, B. crassifolia has magnificent deeply veined round leaves, and bright pink flowers.

Cimicifuga (*Ranunculaceae*) Cimicifuga succeeds well in shade and its slender spires of white flowers can light up a dark corner of the shrubbery. A rather moist soil suits it best.

Dicentra (*Papaveraceae*) The Bleeding Heart, with its pink and white pendant

Above *A strategically placed looking glass makes an enclosed town garden seem twice its size. Framing the "visto" are swags of ivy, and tall plants of bamboo. Arundinaria Murielae is a bamboo which will grow well in semi-shade*

Below *Unusual plants to find on a roof-top garden: a Weeping Willow, Salix babylonica, and the giant hemlock, Heracleum Mantegazzianum*

Opposite *Some roses are good natured (and strong growing) enough to give a fine show of flower even if not planted in direct sunshine. A few which will tolerate a northern aspect, are Félicité et Perpétue, Gloire de Dijon, Maigold and Mme Alfred Carrière (shown here)*

flowers (from which it takes its name) and elegant arching habit is a plant of great character. It naturalizes well in a half shaded border.

Digitalis (*Scrophulariaceae*) Foxgloves are among the best of plants for naturalizing in lightly shaded woodland or semi-sunless borders. The new Excelsior strains with flowers borne all round the stem, instead of only on one side, are a sensational improvement on the type. D. lutea is a worthwhile perennial foxglove, with yellow or white flowers.

Epimedium (*Berberidaceae*) All epimediums are useful plants to grow in shade where their leaves make attractive ground cover. E. grandiflorum Rose Queen, with evergreen foliage and rose pink flowers is a particularly good one. Warleyense, with orange flowers and coppery foliage is another.

Erythronium (*Liliaceae*) Dog's Tooth Violets are attractive plants for a damp, half shaded position, with marbled leaves which are as great an attraction as their flowers. E. Dens-canis has leaves which are parti-coloured in purple and brown, with rose coloured flowers. E. tuolumnense has bright green leaves and yellow flowers.

Fatsia (*Araliaceae*) City gardeners, with shaded gardens and poor soil, will find a real friend in Fatsia japonica, which will

Above *The False Goat's Beard, Astilbe Arendsii, will do well in half-shade, as long as its roots are in soil that is not too dry. The white form, Deutschland, is one of the best to choose*

Below *The Golden Hollies will tolerate some shade and as their leaves are glossy, they readily throw off town dirt. Ilex Aquifolium Golden Queen is one of the brightest*

Opposite above *Azaleas are first class plants for a cool position shaded by trees, though they are not ideal for town gardens*

Below *Almost the most brilliant red in the garden is provided by Lobelia cardinalis, a plant which thrives in deep rich soil, and a corner that is partially shaded from the midday sun*

137

grow almost anywhere. Its glossy palmate evergreen leaves are surmounted in autumn (sometimes as late as November) by umbels of cream coloured flowers.

Fuchsia (*Oenotheraceae*) The hardy fuchsias make the most graceful of shrubs for town gardens. F. gracilis with pink and purple flowers is one of the hardiest. F. thompsonii, of erect growth, is one of the freest flowerers. F. versicolor has attractive variegated foliage, flushed with pink, and deep crimson and purple flowers. F. magellanica Mrs W. P. Wood has the freshest green leaves and pale pink flowers.

Helleborus (*Ranunculaceae*) Most hellebores grow happily in shade, and are endearing in the way they are among the very first garden plants to flower. The Christmas Rose (H. niger) and the Lenten Rose (H. viridis) sometimes even flower before the old year is out. H. foetidus has striking foliage, but of all hellebores, H. corsicus is the most spectacular, bearing its jade green flower heads over well-sculptured foliage. It prefers some sun.

Hosta (*Liliaceae*) Of all plants for the city gardener, hostas are the most useful,

Above *Also from Japan comes the popular Anemone japonica, a plant which brings a welcome reminder of spring in early autumn. The Japanese anemones are happiest in half shade, and a cool position*

Below *Polygonatum multiflorum or Solomon's Seal, is a beautiful, old-fashioned, plant for the north side of the wall, or for a position in woodland. It is indifferent as to soil, but prefers to be away from hot sunshine. Its small white flowers are borne on graceful arching stems*

Opposite above *Sanquisorba canadensis, or Burnet, shows slender spires of creamy flowers over rich tufts of deeply cut foliage. It is at its best in a cool, shaded position*

Below *A plant for the connoisseur from Japan. Kirengeshoma palmata, with well sculpted leaves, and pendant pale yellow flowers on slender black stems. It prefers moist, leaf-mouldy soil and protection from full sunshine*

as they will grow in deep shade and poor soil, though, naturally, they respond gratefully if the ground in which they are to grow is to some extent prepared.

Some of the best hostas are the magnificent H. Sieboldiana, H. Fortunei alba picta with leaves splashed with yellow, H. lancifolia with narrower green leaves and, best of all, H. crispula with leaves piped with white. Recently in Northern Ireland, the author saw a new hosta with pure gold leaves, grown from seed from Japan, which soon should be in commerce, and is a sensational plant. The leaves of hostas are always more interesting than the flowers.

Hydrangea (*Saxifragaceae*) Hydrangeas whose name means water, are all happiest with their roots in cool soil. Of the many forms in commerce, some are outstanding plants, and should be in every garden, especially shaded ones. Of the well known Hortensia group (H. macrophylla Hortensia) the deep red Altona, the pink (or bright blue on acid soils) Holstein, the white Madame Mouilliére and rose pink Vicomtesse de Vibraye are good plants.

Of the species hydrangeas, H. robusta and two climbing hydrangeas, H. integerrima and petiolaris are interesting. Of the attractive lace cap group, Lanarth White (particularly good in town gardens) the grandiflora form of H. paniculata, and H. quercifolia which colours well in autumn are all good. But the two best hydrangeas for any garden are surely the

Above *Foxgloves, Digitalis purpurea, are happiest growing in shaded woodland, where they are generous seeders. The new Excelsior hybrids have fuller flower heads in pink, deep rose, and pale yellow, as well as the usual white and purple*
Below *The Tibetan Poppies are all plants which delight in a cool root-run in soil that is full of peat. The yellow Meconopsis regia, which forms attractive furry rosettes of leaves early in the year, is one of the most impressive*
Opposite *Iris "Opal" luxuriates in the dappled shade provided by an arcade of pleached Acacia bessoniana*

velvet leaved H. Sargentiana and lilac flowered H. villosa.

Kirengeshoma (*Saxifragaceae*) This is a real connoisseur's plant, and ideal to plant in the front of a shrub border or in shady woodland. Its leaves resemble those of a sycamore tree, and it bears its yellow bell – flowers on ebony stems, in late summer.

Meconopsis (*Papaveraceae*) Of all the large poppy family, the prize must surely go to the poppies from the Himalayas, and the best of that splendid group, and the one most likely to succeed in western gardens, is Meconopsis grandis, with bright blue flowers. But these will only be borne if the plant is set in soil it likes – moist, peaty loam, and in half shade. A cross between M. betonicifolia and M. grandis, M. sheldonii, is an excellent perennial poppy, while other Himalayans of great distinction, are M. Dhwojii, with yellow flowers and brown, downy spring leaves; M. Wallichii, not only blue but

Above *Hebes, as recently veronicas have been re-christened, do not all demand full sun. They thrive by the sea, or in the shelter of a wall. H. brachysiphon White Pearl makes a rounded shrub of well-knit foliage and flowers*

Below *Aquilegia: "The columbines are excellent plants for town gardens, their foliage persisting in beauty long after the flowers are past." The new McKana hybrids are a much improved strain*

Opposite above *Smilacina racemosa, a great addition to Western gardens, which originated in North America. Its sweet scented white flowers are borne in feathery heads, and it flourishes in a damp, cool spot*

Below left *Erythronium, Dog's Tooth Violets, are delightful little plants "with marbled leaves which are as great an attraction as their flowers". Their flowers are pink, or yellow, and borne in spring. Also known as Dame's Violet*

Below right *Helleborus niger, the Christmas Rose, if given some protection, will flower in mid-winter. Helleborus orientalis, shown here, the Lenten Rose, flowers in spring, in shades of white or purple*

occasionally red and purple; and the very rare pink M. sherriffii. These are all connoisseurs' plants of the first order.

Pulmonaria (*Boraginaceae*) Two desirable lungworts are P. angustifolia Munstead Blue, with bright blue flowers, and P. saccharata with attractive leaves marbled with silver, and pink and blue flowers. Both like light shade and a damp situation.

Veratrum (*Liliaceae*) In partly shaded moist positions veratrum can show leaves as spectacular as any in the garden; they

Above *A spectacular explosion of leaves provided by Hosta crispula, a shade-plant par excellence*

Above left *Polyanthus grow well in deep moist soil, with leaf mould added and plenty of moisture. Originally a man-made cross between the wild cowslip and the primrose, the polyanthus has recently been further developed to include plants that flower in shades of blue, as well as deep rose*

Below *Primula auricula have fascinating mealy flowers in such unexpected colours as grey, terra-cotta, brown and green, which show up best in half shade. Their culture was a passion in the last century*

Opposite *Verbascum Chaixii rears its candelabra of yellow flowers in late summer – and its flannelly stems can reach a height of six feet or more. A biennal, it seeds about freely. Its colloquial names are mullein, or in ancient times, Hag Taper. Verbascum prefer to grow in a lightly shaded position*

are at their best in spring. Its flowers, either dark red or greenish white, are not attractive.

Viola (*Violaceae*) A personal choice from the hundreds of kinds of violas that there are, would include V. cornuta which bears its blue flowers all summer long, gracilis Martin, deep violet, and the pale yellow V. gracilis Moonlight. Jackanapes has enchanting flowers of chocolate and yellow, with an almost human expression. Viola labradorica will grow in deep shade and has attractive dark purple leaves: it is a great spreader.

Above *All hydrangeas prefer light shade, and especially the large velvet leaved Hydrangea Sargentiana appreciates the protection offered by overhanging trees. Its flowers are white and born in spreading heads of florets. H. Sargentiana was named after the distinguished founder of the Arnold Arboretum in Massachusetts, Charles Sargent (1841–1972)*

Left *Hydrangeas will grow happily in pots, tubs, or as here, an old lead tank, if watered regularly. Their name, hydrangea, is formed of two Greek words, hydor, water and aggeion, a receptacle*

Opposite *Blue Hydrangea hortensia in the garden of Smedmore Manor in Dorset. Hydrangeas vary in colour according to the soil in which they are planted: blue on acid soil, or pink when the soil is alkaline: to the left of the picture can be seen the red spikes of Polygonum amplexicaule*

Waterside

Waterside gardening is a comparatively modern form of gardening, though water itself has always played a great part in the well designed garden; from the fountains of the Moorish garden at the Generalife, to the canals and *piéces d'eau* of the great French gardens of the eighteenth century. But waterside planting - and the culture of water lilies, is a very new idea. Miss Gertrude Jekyll once wrote that anyone who had observed the banks of a river or lake from the intimate point of view of the leisured nature-lover in boat or canoe, "would be struck by the beauty of the native waterside plants; for many of them are among the most pictorial . . ."

Le Nôtre, the designer of Versailles, would have thought the banks of his canals or the rims of his fountains disfigured - if not disgraced - by casual plantings of bulrush or sagittaria; and yet such groupings, if the setting is not too formal, can offer enchanting pictures.

The gardener who has water at his command - either a natural stream or pond, or water artificially contrived, is fortunate indeed.

Water itself introduces another dimension to gardening - acting as looking glasses do in the decoration of a room. It has been said that water in any form in a garden is an advantage, whether in the form of a lake or stream, or a simple rising and falling jet.

The surface of lake, pond or pool can be embellished with

Opposite *A bridge in Chinoiserie style spans the lake at Pusey House in Berkshire, a great English garden open for the public to visit for many months a year. In the left foreground, Lysimachia punctata "presents spires of bright yellow flowers for months on end"*

Right *The lake at Wakehurst Park, decorated on its banks with trees and shrubs of differing shapes and colouring, and on its surface by two interesting specimens of Chenopsis atratus from Australia. The garden at Wakehurst has recently come under the aegis of Kew*

water lilies far more beautiful today than any that Monet had to paint, for no garden plants has been more improved in the last century. But water lilies must be planted right, and it will be found that they will do better by far if the soil in which they are planted covers the whole surface of the pool, rather than being contained in baskets. The operation of planting water lilies can be simplified if the root is put in a "sandwich" of two pieces of turf, and dropped where the plant is to grow. One mistake would-be growers of water lilies often make is to plant them near a fountain. Few water plants like to grow in water that is not still, and, of all flowers, water lilies resent water on their petals, and being rocked about.

There are many plants which grow happily with their feet in water. Plants as different in size and character as the lowly mimulus (the Musk or Monkey Flower, from the supposed likeness of its corolla to a monkey's face) to that giant-leaved waterside plant from Brazil, the gunnera. Marsh Marigold, the poetic Japanese Iris and the yellow and purple loosestrifes, are all plants which love to grow by, or in water.

But when the margins of your pool or stream are planted, Robert Harling has a word of advice, "Don't overlook the necessity for a good garden seat at the waterside. Here is the one place where the cares of the world can be exorcised. But it is surprising how many people forget this essential complement to water's soothing and smoothing balms."

A peaceful resting place like that would have pleased Monet, who painted such beautiful pictures of water lilies and the reflections of the sky and clouds as glimpsed between their shining lily-pads. It has been said that water lilies seem to have a mute message, and that Monet was able to pass it on to us.

Above *"Water . . . introduces another dimension to gardening, acting as looking glasses do in the decoration of a room."* The fountain pool in the garden at Hungerdown House in Wiltshire
Left *Rhododendrons delight in a position near water where there is a cool root-run and moisture continually in the air*
Right *"Waterside plants . . . are among the most pictorial of all"*

Inspired planting by the waterside in a garden in France. Among the noticeable plants are Osmunda regalis, the Royal Fern, called after Osmunder, a Scandinavian god in remote times, and Peltiphyllum peltatum, the Umbrella Plant, with its bouquets of shining leaves: tucked away on the far left hand side of the picture can be discerned the narrow leaves of Sagittaria sagittifolia

153

Arum (*Araceae*) Arum Lilies, or Zante-deschia, are hardier than they were once thought, and will grow well, if planted by the waterside, or better still, actually in shallow water, where their roots are protected from frost.

Astilbe (*Saxifragaceae*) There are very few astilbes really worth garden space. But Fanal – bright crimson, the drought resisting Federsee, and pink A. Arendsii, are good plants. Most astilbes prefer to be planted in a moist situation.

Doronicum (*Compositae*) The Leopard's Banes show their golden daisy flowers early in the year. Spring Beauty is a good new variety. Though easy-going they prefer a damp situation.

Above *Iris pseudacorus folius variagatus shows slender swordlike leaves of palest gold in spring, which darken to green as summer passes*

Above right *Grasses like Eulalia sinensis variegatus associate well with water; with their roots reaching down to the moisture beneath, they quickly made graceful fountains of leaves*

Below *Hemerocallis, or Day Lilies delight in growing by water, as these, on the bank of a lily-padded lake*

Opposite *A formal pool with its edges softened by foliage in contrasting forms*

Gunnera (*Haloragidaceae*) Gunnera is the most imposing of all plants for the waterside, and no plant can produce such giant leaves – but as it comes from Brazil, gunnera needs some winter protection, such as a covering of its own dead leaves – G. manicata is the best variety.

Hemerocallis (*Liliaceae*) Recently these have been much developed and improved, and there are now Day Lilies to be had in colours unknown fifty years ago. A few of the best and most brightly coloured, are the rose Pink Damask, the vermilion Rajah, the lemon yellow Vespers and the dark brown Bagette – Morocco Beauty has flowers that are

almost purple. One of the beauties of hemerocallis is its graceful luminous spring foliage.

Lysichitum (*Araceae*) The Skunk Cabbages add an exotic luxurious note to any waterside planting, and delight in a damp situation and deep soil. L. camtschatcense, from Siberia, is smaller, and its trumpet shaped flowers are white.

Lysimachia (*Primulaceae*) By the waterside, Lysimachia punctata presents spires of bright yellow flowers for months on end.

Mimulus (*Scrophulariacae*) Of all the Musks – M. cardinalis would seem the most desirable. Its scarlet flowers persist

Above *Some hostas – or Plantain Lilies, have more impressive flowers than others. Here H. plantaginea grandiflora complacently observes its reflection in the water*

Right *Gunnera manicata, from Brazil, will over-winter well, if its plant-crowns are covered with its own dead leaves, or with straw*

Opposite *The lush leaves of Bergenia cordifolia and the large ones of Rheum palmatum atropurpureum, the ornamental rhubarb; this plant, contrary to popular belief, prefers not to be planted with its roots in water, but in a position well up on the water's bank*

for months on end and, its foliage remains fresh and attractive. An ideal plant for a damp soil.

Nymphaea (*Nymphaeaceae*) There are several water lilies which are so outstandingly better plants than others that their names should be carefully noted. These are the splendid white gladstoniana, the rich rose-coloured Mrs Richmond, the crimson James Brydon, and Golden Sunrise. For the connoisseur who will take the trouble to give it the special care it needs (raising, drying and wintering indoors) N. caerulea – Blue Beauty, is a beautiful blue water lily.

Nyssa (*Nyssaceae*) Nyssa sylvatica, the Tupelo, offers the brightest autumn colours imaginable and loves to be planted in acid soil preferably near water. After all, the tree's name derives from Nyssa, a Greek water nymph.

"The surface of lake, pond or pool can be embellished with water lilies far more beautiful today, than any that Monet had to paint." James Brydon has flowers of rich crimson, while Mrs Richmond is rose-coloured. Gladstoniana is the largest of all white water lilies, with flowers which are sometimes ten inches across. Marliacea chromatella is a beautiful clear yellow, with marbled leaves

159

Peltiphyllum (*Saxifragaceae*) Peltiphyllum peltatum has large handsome leaves and rose coloured sprays of flowers – it likes a position near water where it soon makes a luxuriant clump of foliage.

Rodgersia (*Saxifragaceae*) The rodgersias make striking waterside plants, though they will grow well in any position that is not too dry. The pinnata hybrids with their differing leaf forms and rosy flowers, are the ones to look for.

Sagittaria (*Alismataceae*) Aquatic plants of great character, the Arrow Heads (from their arrow shaped leaves) are of the easiest culture. They are subjects rather for the stream or lakeside than for the formal pool.

Above *In the pool in the great Scottish Botanic garden at Logan, Wigtownshire, grows the Water Hawthorn Aponogeton distachyus, with sweetly scented flowers. In the background can be seen the fronded tufts of tree ferns, Dicksonia antarctica*

Opposite above *The unfolding croziers of waterside fern Osmunda regalis by the lake at Scotney Castle – an important Sussex garden open to the public under the National Trust*

Opposite below *Caltha palustris – the old-fashioned Marsh Marigold, is still one of the most spectacular plants for the waterside. Alba is a single white form, while C. flore pleno has double butter-yellow flowers*

Spiraea (*Rosaceae*) Few of the spiraeas are worthy of garden room. The most often met with, S. arguta – "Bridal Wreath" – and S. japonica perhaps having been much planted in recent years. But S. japonica alpina is an attractive miniature shrub, and the much taller S. nipponica rotundifolia is useful in that it will grow on chalk. Its white flowers are very showy. Best of all the spiraeas is probably S. Veitchii of which the cool white flowers are specially welcome in July.

Trollius (*Ranunculaceae*) Of the several trollius or Globe Flowers in cultivation, Canary Bird and the orange flowered Prichard's Giant are the ones to look for.

Above *Yellow Primula Florindae has sulphur yellow flowers, and is a prolific seeder. It was named after the well known plants-woman Florinda Norman Thompson*
Right *Primula japonica has flowers in rosy-pink tiers. It likes to have its feet in water, and flower-heads in the sun*
Opposite *Astilbes and primulas make a luxuriant edging to a willow-shaded lake. Fanal is a bright red astilbe – A. Arendsii (in the foreground) a pleasing soft pink*

Above "*Arum Lilies – or zantedeschia – are hardier than they were once thought, and will grow well if planted by the waterside, or better still, actually in shallow water, where their roots are protected from frost*"

Left *The white form of lysichitum – L. camtschatcense, originates in Siberia, and is rarer than the yellow L. americanum, the Skunk Cabbage* **opposite**

Colour

The colour of a garden - like that of Austin Dobson's Phyllida "comes and goes" in spring, in summer it "trembles to a lily and it wavers to a rose," and in autumn it fairly blazes; but it is a dying fire, and in a few weeks it has gone. And the colour of a garden is so precious that it should be sedulously preserved, and prolonged for as long as possible. The colours available in flowers and foliage are innumerable, but however brilliant, if they are arranged badly, they are, in the words of that great gardener, Miss Gertrude Jekyll "like a box of paints from the best colourman . . . or to go one step further, it is like portions of these paints set out upon a palette. This does not constitute a picture."

And Miss Jekyll goes on to say, "It is just in the way it is done that lies the difference between common-place gardening and gardening that may rightly claim to rank as a fine art. Given the same space of ground and the same material, they may be either fashioned into a dream of beauty . . . a series of soul satisfying pictures . . . or they may be so misused that everything is jarring . . ." In the spacious days of Miss Jekyll, colour in the garden really meant the colour of flowers, the colour of the lily and of the rose.

Today the thoughtful, though overworked, gardener looks for colour not only in flower, but also in leaf. For the most must be made of every moment of the year that is not winter. And even then, the resourceful gardener can now find plants with leaves to cheer the dimmest days. The colour comes and goes, but today if a garden is carefully planned, it need not go completely. The golden holly, the gilded leaves of elaeagnus, the warm silver of lavender, and the blue tints of the leaves of rue, can lighten the border, and comfort the eye even at Christmas. Important pages of this book are devoted to such plants, for it seems that the careful use of plants with coloured foliage is one of the most significant developments in modern gardening. And the gardener who can combine flower and leaf colour effectively, is a gardener indeed.

Above *The luminous flowers of tulip White Triumphator light up a shady shrub border*
Opposite *A burst of colour in the famous bulb garden at Springfields near Spalding, England's answer to Holland's Keukenhof. Grape hyacinths, Muscari armeniacum, crimson tulip Cassini, gold trumpeted daffodils and yellow doronicum set the scene*

Abelia (*Caprifoliaceae*) Abelia is a half hardy shrub, with attractive pink flowers, which needs a sheltered position and full sun. A. grandiflora is the strongest variety.

Abutilon (*Malvaceae*) The half hardy Indian Mallow, Abutilon megapotamicum, presents rich flowers of yellow and crimson in late summer. A. vitifolium with blue flowers is hardy in a sheltered position in the South.

Acacia (*Leguminosae*) The Rose Acacia has attractive pink flowers and ferny foliage. Pseudacacia (Robinia) Frisia shows leaves of golden yellow and is a most attractive small tree. But, like all acacias, its branches are brittle.

Ageratum (*Compositae*) This half hardy annual shows its powdery blue flowers from June onwards. Blue Mink is the best variety.

Alstroemeria (*Amaryllidaceae*) The Herb Lilies offer splendid colour in summer, though some varieties, such as aurantiaca and brasiliensis are almost too brash. The Ligtu Hybrids, however, from Peru, are subtler in shade, and excellent for cutting.

Althaea (*Malvaceae*) Hollyhocks – the epitome of cottage flowers – perhaps should not find a place in a book on plants for the connoisseur, but the annual Indian Spring and Indian Summer strains

Left *Late summer colour in the border provided by yellow dahlias and tall pink Michaelmas Daisy, Festival, with the lower growing Jenny in front. Left, the dew-frosted leaves of herbaceous Geranium Endressii*

Below *In another part of the same border, are soaring rudbeckias – pink Japanese anemone Kriemhilde, Sedum spectabile and the blue leaves of Ruta graveolens Jackman's Blue*

Opposite *Many coloured bearded iris at the base of a sun-baked wall. In the foreground, the golden Rajah, with the rich purple Dark Fury beyond. Tip for successful iris growing: "lots of old mortar rubble, cut the leaves right back after flowering, and divide clumps every three years"*

might be of interest to lovers of simple flowers, for if sown under glass in early spring, they will flower generously in August, and in the most alluring shades of rose-pink.

Amaranthus (*Amaranthaceae*) Love Lies Bleeding makes a colourful annual with its long tassels of scarlet flowers. The white form is a good looking plant too. Both flower in late summer and are raised readily from seed.

Amaryllis (*Amaryllidaceae*) Belladonna lilies do well in a well-drained warm position at the base of a wall. A. Belladonna is rose-coloured and sweet-smelling. The greenhouse varieties, in different colours, and sometimes striped, are known as hippeastrum.

Anchusa (*Boraginaceae*) The borages, or alkanets, show some of the most brilliant blue flowers of summer. Morning Glory, and the award winning caespitosa Loddon Royalist are two good hybrids. Opal is an attractive pale blue. Anchusa myosotidiflora, in moist soil, looks like a rather grand Forget-me-not, and does well in half shade.

Antirrhinum (*Scrophulariaceae*) There are endless varieties of snapdragons to grow from seed, or buy as young plants from the nurseryman. Two plants for the connoisseur are A. Asarina with yellow flowers and a creeping habit, and glutinosum with creamy flowers, sticky foliage and a liking for rockwork.

Aster (*Compositae*) Michaelmas Daisies, Aster novi-belgii, with their starry flowers

Above *The early spring leaves of Pieris forrestii Wakehurst are brighter than any flower*
Right above *Pure white Lilium regale*
Below *Coronado hybrid lily Enchantment, with orange-red flowers*
Opposite *Three plants for the connoisseur in one picture. Two euphorbias, the yellow E. polychroma and the orange bracted E. griffithii Fireglow, grow in the shelter of a wall curtained with pink Clematis vedrariensis rosea*

in a dozen different shades of purple, pink, red and blue, provide a galaxy of colour at the end of summer. A few for the connoisseur might well include Crimson Brocade, the best red yet, the purple red Gayborder Royal, pink Festival, low growing pink Jenny, and powder blue Marie Ballard. Winston Churchill has dark red flowers which are almost beetroot in colour.

Astrantia (*Umbelliferae*) The Masterworts make good border plants with their greenish flowers. A. carniolica major has spherical flowers faintly shaded with pink.

Auricula (*Primulaceae*) Auriculas have been specialists' plants for many years and there were Auricula Societies all over the North of England and Scotland in the 18th century. Show auriculas, such as the green edged Greenfinch and the grey petalled Grey Friar, to name but two, need very special treatment and culture, but the hardier kinds, such as Golden Gleam, Gordon Douglas and Pink Lady will grow well in any open, well drained, not too warm, position.

Caryopteris (*Verbenaceae*) Caryopteris clandonensis is the best hybrid, and is quite hardy in a well-drained sunny position: it has lanceolate leaves and flowers of electric blue in autumn. C. tangutica is even hardier.

All caryopteris should be pruned back in spring.

Left. *The cool tones of buddleia Peace sets off the warmer colouring of pink phlox and scarlet Lobelia cardinalis in a Scottish border*
Opposite above *Delphiniums and the flat headed flowers of Achillea Eupatorium Gold Plate. Lavender-bordered steps lead down to a garden with floribunda roses, Iceberg*
Below left *Delphiniums and hemerocallis on the edge of a shrubbery*
Below right *More Iceberg roses in a herbaceous border. In the foreground is that excellent salvia – S. superba, of which the deep purple flower spires persist for weeks on end in late summer*

174

Catananche (*Compositae*) The herbaceous C. caerulea is the best form of catananche and shows crisp blue papery flowers in June. The ancient Greeks used catananche in love-potions.

Celmisia (*Compositae*) The celmisias originated in New Zealand and make attractive plants for the well drained border or rock-garden. C. argentea and C. ramulosa are very special plants, as is the large flowered C. Hookeri.

Ceratostigma (*Plumbaginaceae*) One of the best of all small shrubs for colour in late summer, ceratostigma bears its blue flowers over a long period from July onwards. Its brown seed heads are attractive too. Though quite hardy, it is a plant which usually dies down to the ground in winter – but quickly grows again in spring.

Cytisus (*Leguminosae*) C. Battandieri, the Moroccan Broom, a shrub with silvery leaves and cone shaped flower heads, which some think smell of pineapples, and some of quince. It does well against a high wall.

C. burkwoodii has flowers of crimson. C. scoparius (The Common Broom) in its form Cornish Cream, has flowers of a colour which its name well describes. Dorothy Walpole is a rich dark red. C. kewensis is low growing and sulphurflowered. C. atropurpureus has deep purple flowers in May.

Dahlia (*Compositae*) Some connoisseurs may sniff at the dahlia, but no plant offers such a generous range of colours, and so many flowers for so long – from

Right *No plant family has such a wide range of brilliant colouring as dahlias. Raiser's Pride is a cactus-flowered dahlia with coral-coloured, quilled petals*

Opposite *Bergamot, Monarda didyma strikes a bold note of red in June and July. Cambridge Scarlet is one of the brightest*

July till the first frosts. Some of the best – from the point of view of habit, foliage, richness of colour, and character, are the large flowered maroon Adolph Mayer, the mauve Lavender Perfection and the purple Town Topic. Of the smaller flowered decorative dahlias the favourite pink flowered Gerrie Hoek is still outstanding – as is the pale gold Glorie Van Heemstede and the orange Prairie Fire.

The cactus and pompon type of dahlia are not perhaps to be considered as flowers of the first choice – nor are the collarettes – but the new Elstead Strains provide attractive flower and leaf colour for the gardener who would plan his borders with an eye for originality. And those two old favourites, the deep purple white tipped Deuil du Roi Albert, and red flowered winey-leaved Bishop of Llandaff, are two dahlias without which any garden would be the poorer.

Delphinium (*Ranunculaceae*) It is difficult to think of the delphinium as being a relation of the butter-cup, but they belong to the same family. Of the many splendid border delphiniums Anne Page, the black-bee'd Harvest Moon, the lilac mauve Lady Dorothy, rich purple blue Sir Neville Pearson and the fine new white Mollie Hanson are five fine flowers. More unusual is the Belladonna Delphinium Ruysii, Pink Sensation, the first pure pink worth growing, the giant flowered Pacific Strains, and the exquisite Blue Butterfly which flowers its first year from seed and grows no more than 12 inches high.

1 Herbaceous Geranium macrorrhizum, close leaved, with rosy flowers. 2 Clematis chrysocoma has flowers of pale ivory. 3 Azalea mollis comes in shades varying from coral to cream. 4 Clematis Lasurstern has starry flowers of purple-blue. 5 The climbing potato, Solanum crispum autumnale, has sprays of purple yellow-centred potato flowers
Opposite *Dahlias make a bonfire of burning colours from July until the first frosts*

Dictamnus (*Rutaceae*) The 'Burning Bush' has flowers of rosy red, and aromatic foliage. It has been growing in European gardens since the reign of Queen Elizabeth. Dictamnus has a curious combustible quality, hence its popular name; it will burst into quick flame if, on a warm still evening, a match is held to its leaves and stem, the plant being quite unharmed by this odd manifestation. D. Fraxinella is the variety to grow.

Dracocephalum (*Labiatae*) The Dragon Flower, or sometimes Obedient Plant, is an addition to any border, with its lilac flowers which are shown at their best in partial shade. The leaves and flowers of the Obedient Plant have a curious characteristic, hence its pseudonym, of remaining in any position into which they are moved. D. Ruyschianum is the best variety.

Echinops (*Compositae*) The Globe Thistles are the hardiest of perennials, and thrive in any sunny, well drained border. Taplow Blue shows round heads of metallic blue in July and is as good as any.

Echium (*Boraginaceae*) The giant blue echiums of Southern and Mediterranean gardens are not for colder climates – but one annual echium – Blue Bedder – is an admirable plant, and if planted in situ in April and thinned out later will flower from July till autumn. There are Vipers Bugloss' in shades of pink, mauve and

Above *Sweet William, Dianthus barbatus lays a magic carpet of colour in June. On the arch, rose Madame Gregoire Staechlin*
Below *The lush petals of Peace roses seem gilded by the evening sun*
Opposite above *Dianthus barbatus. In the foreground the old favourite auricula-eyed variety, with flowers of white, with a crimson centre*
Below left *A border of mixed phlox*
Below right *The seldom grown Dictamnus Fraxinella purpureus, dittany or Burning Bush. Its leaves and stem exhale an inflammable oil which, if a match is applied, will momentarily ignite, leaving the plant quite unharmed*

white, as well as blue.

Erigeron (*Compositae*) The erigerons make low cushions of daisy flowers and are useful for cutting. Three good varieties are the violet Dignity, the light blue, yellow centred Sincerity, and bright pink Vanity. All should be cut down after flowering, to preserve the plant's neat form.

Erythrina (*Leguminosae*) The Coral Tree has an exotic appearance, and its bright red flowers fairly blaze in mid-

Above *Ivy-leaved geraniums are the pot plant par excellence, as seen here, growing in an old stone vase*

Below *Hydrangea macrophylla brings tones of pink and pale blue to the garden in late summer*

Opposite *Peonies are the glory of the garden in June. Duchesse de Nemours (above) is creamy white. M. Jules Elie, large flowered, with petals of silvery pink. Peonies, once planted, should, if possible, never be disturbed*

summer. E. crista galli (Cock's Comb) is the one to grow. All erythinas need the warmest and most sheltered position possible.

Escallonia (*Saxifragaceae*) Escallonias are some of the best natured of flowering evergreens and are not particular as to soil or situation. They grow well by the sea. A few of the best are C. F. Ball with crimson flowers, the long flowering Donard Brilliance, E. G. Cheeseman with bell-shaped cherry coloured flowers, and Peach Blossom, pale pink. And for gardeners in search of something out of the ordinary, there is E. illinita, with white flowers and an odd, but not unpleasant, smell of the farmyard.

Festuca (*Gramineae*) The blue-green Fescue grass provides a subtle touch of coloured foliage wherever it is planted. It does well in full sun and light sandy soil. To be fully effective, its tufts should be planted closely together, to form a mat.

Forsythia (*Oleaceae*) Of the popular forsythias three are outstandingly superior to the others. Intermedia Lynwood, primulina (with softer yellow flowers) and ovata tetragold, a smaller shrub than the type, and better suited to the smaller garden.

Helianthus (*Compositae*) The annual sunflower is surely one of the noblest of flowers, rarity or not. And there are perennial helianthus which are almost as effective, such as the opulent double Soleil d'Or and the imposing Monarch.

Heucherella (*Saxifragaceae*) This is a cross between heuchera (called after the German botanist Johann Heucher) and tiarella. Bridget Bloom, with neat rosettes of dark leaves and long-lasting sprays of light pink flowers is the variety to look for.

Hibiscus (*Malvaceae*) The shrubby mallows are very useful, colourful plants for gardeners on chalk. Hibiscus syriacus Blue Bird, Duc de Brabant (double red), Hamabo (white with a crimson patch), and Woodbridge (rose pink) are four of the best.

Hypericums (*Guttiferae*) are good natured as to soil, and their golden flowers are a joy in July and August. But there are so many that it is important to plant only the best varieties. These should certainly include the shade tolerant Androsaemum with flowers that are followed by spectacular seed-vessels, H. patulum Hidcote with the largest flowers of all; the good cushion-forming olympicum, H. Moserianum tricolor with leaves parti-coloured in green, pink, and perhaps the best hypericum of them all, Rowallane, named for a great garden in Northern Ireland, which can grow to a height of six feet in a sheltered position. H. frondosum, which makes a miniature tree, is another attractive hypericum.

Iris (*Iridaceae*) There are iris in as many colours as the rainbow from which they take their name. The bearded iris are the showiest, and it would be difficult to exceed in garden value such hybrids as Golden Rajah, Blue Ensign, the chartreuse-green Cleo, pale blue Jane Phillips and flamingo pink Party Dress. But more refined by far are the species iris. Iris such as the sky-blue winter flowering unguicularis (especially in its superba form) and I. cristata lacustris, pale blue and golden centred. I. foetidissima, a shade lover, is mainly grown for its bright autumn seeds which show up well in their bursting pods. I. Kaempferi is the Japanese Iris, which loves to grow by water. Two of the loveliest, and strangest, of species iris, are I. tuberosa (or Hermodactylus tuberosus) with green and black flowers, and the exotic I. susiana which has grey petals streaked with black.

Kniphofia (*Liliaceae*) Kniphofia, Tritoma or Red Hot Poker is a plant which has brightened Western gardens since the reign of Queen Anne. There are many new varieties which are an improvement on the type – Royal Standard, the pale yellow Buttercup and the golden flowered, short growing Goldelse are all good plants – while the species K. caulescens, with leaves as exotic as an agaves, is specially imposing. All kniphofias must have sharp drainage, and on heavy soil should be planted on slightly raised ground.

Joseph Joubert was of the opinion that tulips, unlike roses or lilies, had no soul. But soul or no, tulips certainly provide brighter and more varied colour than any other spring flower
Above *Yellow tulips bring a gleam of sunlight to a terraced city garden*
Opposite *The garden at Abbey Leix in Ireland*

Blue as a colour is of the greatest value in a garden. On these two pages are shown three borders in which blue is the predominant shade

Kolkwitzia (*Caprifoliaceae*) Kolkwitzia, the Beauty Bush so popular in American gardens, is of the easiest cultivation and not particular as to soil. Pink Cloud is a good new variety with brighter flowers than the type.

Lathyrus (*Leguminosae*) The Everlasting Pea has grown in Western gardens for centuries. The usual magenta purple flowered variety is not perhaps a plant for the connoisseur, but L. rubellum with rosy pink flowers, and the new White Pearl are attractive climbers. All lathyrus are deep rooting, and resent disturbance.

Lobelia (*Campanulaceae*) There are lobelias which are very different from the plants one sees all too often, used as an edging, alternating with white candy-tuft. Though lobelias, if planted in masses and close together, as that great gardener Victoria Sackville West, advised, can be effective enough.

The perennial L. cardinalis – with brilliant red flowers and wine-dark foliage is a splendid plant. L. vedrariensis has mauve flowers and green leaves, and L. syphilitica is light blue.

Lupinus (*Leguminosae*) Lupins have recently lost the popularity they enjoyed some years ago. Their flowering season is short – their leaves are untidy (they should not be cut down until the autumn), and as plants they are short lived. But at their best, some of the Russell strains are

Above *Campanula persicifolia Telham Beauty: in front, the glossy leaves of Bergenia cordifolia, one of the best of plants for the front of a border*
Below *A blue and white border at Chatsworth, greatest of the great houses of England. The cool colour scheme is made up of delphiniums, white nicotiana; a datura to the right, and in the foreground, one of the best of all annuals, Echium Blue Bedder, an excellent garden form of Vipers Bugloss*
Opposite *Delphiniums and Campanula persicifolia Blue Belle, reflect the steely colouring of the branches of Cedrus atlantica glauca, the Blue Cedar*

lovely things. Blushing Bride, the oddly coloured Josephine, which has flowers of slatey blue and lemon, the blue and white Lady Diana Abdy, and dusky Thunder-cloud, are all great flowers.

The Tree Lupin, Lupinus arboreus, if naturalized in full sun will flower for months on end, and generously seed itself about; it is a plant of great character. The seldom grown L. Chamissonis is a real plant for the connoisseur. It has attractive grey foliage and mauve flowers in May.

Lychnis (*Caryophyllaceae*) There are several Rose Campions which make excellent border plants, L. Flos Jovis, in both its crimson and white flowered forms, and L. Flos Jovis (Sir John Hort's variety) which makes a smaller plant with pleasing pink flowers above silver leaves. Lychnis Haageana has red leaves and red flowers.

Malva (*Malvaceae*) There are a few mallows which the discriminating gardener might well plant, especially if his garden is on chalk or very limey soil: Malva fastigiata is an imposing plant with flowers of clear pink, and the annual malope offers flowers of different shades of crimson, white and flesh over a long period.

Oenothera (*Onagraceae*) The Evening Primrose flowers from June until autumn, and the type will seed itself generously. Two to look for are Fireworks (O. fyverkeri) and Yellow River.

Paeonia (*Ranunculaceae*) Border peonies are among the great beauties of the garden in June and there is little to choose between the many different hybrids offered. In fact a certain sameness, except in colour, among the best of border peonies, such as the pink Clara Dubois, the white Duchesse de Nemours, Lady Alexandra Duff and Sarah Bernhardt, could be considered a weakness. But this certainly cannot be said for species peonies which all have great character and differ widely in colour and form. Some of the best are P. obovata with white flowers and golden stamens, P. emodi with deeply cut foliage and papery flowers, peregrina lobata with

The golden promises of spring
Above *Tulips in the formal setting of the garden at miniature Kew Palace, formerly known as the Dutch House*
Opposite *Golden cascades of Laburnum Vossii in the garden of Kew Palace*

brilliant carmine flowers, and the crimson flowered lacy-leafed, tenuifolia. Most beautiful of all species peonies perhaps is P. Mlokosewitchi with flowers of clear yellow.

Tree peonies are also plants for the discerning gardener, and there are few more totally handsome plants, handsome in flower, in foliage and in architectural form, as the wine-coloured P. Delavayi, or the yellow flowered P. lutea ludlowi.

Papaver (*Papaveraceae*) Few of the Oriental Poppies can claim to be plants for the connoisseur. Their colours are brash, their foliage coarse and their flowering period short. Plant them in a border or you will have patches of ugly green from June until October. But the apricot pink Mrs Perry or Perry's White do have attractive flowers.

For the rock garden there is P. alpinum, of which the yellow flowers and lacy silver leaves are in perfect harmony; and the so-called peony-flowered annual poppies look marvellously opulent.

Penstemon (*Scrophulariaceae*) P. barbatus Torreyi is a very special plant with bright scarlet flowers, as has P. pinifolius with leaves like heather. P. Scouleri makes a delightful neat bush, covered with large mauve flowers in early summer while P. Hartwegii Garnet, with its dark wine flowers is the hardiest of all.

Perovskia (*Labiatae*) Perovskia atriplicifolia shows blue flowers on pearly white stems, and silvery foliage in July and August. It does best in a warm situation and in well-drained soil – Blue

1 *Salvia turkistanica and verbascum in a closely planted, well-sheltered border.* 2 *Pink and white shrub roses and floribundas make a tapestry of soft colour.* 3 *Delphiniums, Nepeta Six Hills Giant and Shasta daisies*
Opposite *Twin borders, set with massed pinks and pansies, in the garden at Cranborne Manor in Dorset, where John Tradescant, afterwards gardener to the Stuart kings, once worked*

Spire is a particularly good variety with larger flowers.

Phlox (*Polemoniaceae*) Phlox decussata which can be the glory of the border from July until September, only do really well in a cool and damp situation. They dislike chalk.

The almost blue Caroline Van Den Berg, the delicate Mother of Pearl, Orange Perfection, and Scarlet Starfire, are all first class flowerers.

For the rock garden there are several very special phlox; P. amoena variegata has variegated leaves, Blue Saucer and May Snow are two of the best of the P. Douglasii, and P. subulata Temiscaming is outstanding.

Potentilla (*Rosaceae*) Potentillas are the best natured of plants – lime tolerant, and though they prefer sun, most will put up with some shade. They flower for months on end. Some of the best are P. fruticosa arbuscula, which is low growing and has golden flowers; beesii with silver leaves and rich yellow flowers; the large flowered Katherine Dykes, and the white mandshurica. Tangerine has unusual orange flowers, which colour best in light shade. The tallest potentilla (six feet sometimes) is the ivory flowered Vilmoriniana.

For the rock garden P. Tonguei, with apricot flowers that are scarlet centred and the tiny P. verna nana, which makes a mat of golden flowers in April, are most desirable little plants.

Best of the herbaceous potentillas is the cherry red P. nepalensis Miss Willmott, which worthily commemorates a great gardener.

Pyracantha (*Rosaceac*) The Firethorns are of the easiest cultivation, and grow in almost any kind of soil. They are excellent wall-coverers in town gardens and

Left *Vividly coloured antirrhinums in a setting of topiary*
Opposite *Lupins, poppies and brilliant daisy-like Pyrethrum roseum, with a closely cropped hornbeam hedge for background*

Above *Papaver orientale – Oriental Poppies are now to be had in far subtler colours than the brash scarlet that one knows too well. Mrs Perry in a delicate pink*

Far left *Alstroemeria is an ordinary enough herbaceous plant, but the new Ligtu hybrids, from Peru, are to be had in fascinating shades of azalea, tangerine rose-colour and even violet*

Left *Leptospermum scoparium Nicholsii, the Manuka tree, from New Zealand, is feathery-leaved, and has sprays of crimson flowers, but it is only for very favoured gardens*

Opposite left *Centaurea macrophala is a large headed thistle with handsome yellow flowers*

Right *Two herbaceous plants which bring bright colour to the border are Galega officinalis, one of the best of the Goats Rues, and Salvia superba, with flowers of cardinalatic purple, followed by decorative bronze coloured seed heads. It was formerly called S. virgata nemorosa. Lubeca in a specially compact form*

their berries (their great beauty), are seldom eaten by birds. Some of the best are atalantioides, which needs little or no sun and berries freely; atalantioides flava, with yellow berries; the robust Lalandei, and the brilliant orange fruited Orange Glow.

Pyrus (*Rosaceae*) Of all the decorative pears by far the most desirable is the silvery Willow Leafed Pear, P. salicifolia, which is unusual in that it seems to exist only in a weeping form.

Rhazya (*Apocynaceae*) The blue flowered rhazya (called after an Arab physician) is a herbaceous plant which is seldom planted, though it has a certain distinction. Once established it is difficult to

move, as it is a deep rooter.

Romneya (*Papaveraceae*) There is not much to choose between the two romneyas most often offered – R. Coulteri and R. trichocalyx – but the American hybrid White Cloud is said to be an improvement on both. Californian Tree Poppies are best grown in free standing beds, rather than at the base of warm walls, which is where they are usually planted. They do well by the sea.

Rubus (*Rosaceae*) Only two of the ornamental brambles seem worthy to be

included in a list of really choice plants. R. Cockburnianus (or giraldianus) for its waxy stems; R. phoenicolasius for its ruddy stems and delicious fruit. The much grown R. tridel – a cross between R. deliciosus and R. trilobus – with its short flowering period and untidy habit

Above *A border of plants chosen for contrasting foliage as well as for flower colour, at Easton Grey in Wiltshire, designed by Peter Coats. Among the plants are bergenia, red leaved Berberis nana and*

blue leaved Ruta graveolens Jackmans blue
Opposite above *Euphorbia Wulfenii and Alstroemeria Ligtu Hybrids bring colour to a London garden*
Below left *Yellow daisy-flowered Senecio Greyii on either side of an old lead tank*
Centre *To supplement a stone carving, seventeenth century but with a definitely modern feeling, the large glaucous blue-green leaves of Hosta sielboldiana elegans*
Right *A paved edging to the lawn makes for easy mowing. In the pot, pink geranium Anna*

of growth, seems an overrated shrub.

Rudbeckia (*Compositae*) The rudbeckias are a brassy, rather common lot, but the new double Goldquelle and green coned Herbstsonne have some distinction, as has the reddish-mauve purpurea.

Sambucus (*Caprifoliaceae*) Sambucus canadensis maxima is one of the best of the elders, and has extra large flowers, with showy dark reddish stems. Other good varieties are S. nigra aurea, one of the best of all yellow leaved shrubs; the ferny leaved S. n. laciniata and S. racemosa plumosa aurea with lacy foliage of the purest gold.

Thalictrum (*Ranunculaceae*) There are at least three Meadow Rues which deserve a place in the gardens of the discerning gardeners – T. aquilegifolium purpureum with fluffy heads of mauve flowers and delicate foliage, the airy T. dipterocarpum with wiry graceful stems and mauve flowers, and T. flavum with striking glaucous leaves and bright yellow flowers.

Tigridia (*Iridaceae*) Tigridias are some of the most exotic border plants that one can grow, with spectacular but short-lived flowers. They need a sunny well drained position and their corms should be hung up in bags in an airy frostproof place, safe from mice, whose favourite diet they seem to be.

Left *A subtly planned border in different greens, greys and whites, with the purple leaves of Perilla frutescens nankinensis for vivid contrast*

Below *A rose garden, with borders surrounded by low hedges of Santolina Chamaecyparissus or Cotton Lavender*

Opposite top left *The rich purple spikes of lavender*

Top right *Wallflower Eastern Queen, a too seldom planted variety, has pink, parti-coloured flowers*

Bottom left *Twin borders of summer flowers in a silver framework of Cotton Lavender*

Bottom right *Pale yellow Hemerocallis citrina with a planting of coral-plumed Bocconia cordata, behind*

Tradescantia (*Commelinaceae*) An old fashioned border flower which gets its name from John Tradescant, gardener to the Stuart Kings of England. Three good forms are rubra (red), T. virginica, J. C. Weguelin (lavender blue), and Osprey (white).

Tulip (*Liliaceae*) There is no better loved flower than the tulip, but there are literally so many thousand different kinds of Darwins, lily-flowered, Rembrandts, Parrots, and Bartigan tulips that choice is difficult for the least demanding connoisseur. However, twelve of the author's favourites would be Keizerskroon, Prince

Above *Hydrangea villosa bears its flowers in late summer*

Left *Lilies, Sedum spectabile, Spiraea Bumalda Anthony Waterer and Day Lilies in a leafy setting*

Opposite *Floribunda rose, Plentiful, under-planted with white and blue pansies in a garden corner which distils the very essence of a summer's day*

of Austria, Van der Neer, Purity, Rijnland, Mount Tacoma, Fantasy, Parrot Wonder, General Eisenhower, Mrs Moon, China Pink, and Queen of Sheba.

With the species tulips it is a different story. Some of these are very special flowers and are not as often planted as they deserve to be. Some of the most attractive are the white and crimson Lady Tulip – T. Clusiana, the white and green T. tarda (though one of the earliest to flower) and the eye-catching, scarlet T. Eichleri. Loveliest of all perhaps, is T. sylvestris with several nodding pale yellow flowers on one stem, a real connoisseur's plant, and said to have been introduced into the West by the Crusaders.

Weigela (*Caprifoliaceae*) Three species weigelas for the connoisseur are W. florida foliis purpureis with pink flowers and purple leaves, W. variegata with parti-coloured leaves, an excellent shrub, and the unusual yellow W. Middendorfiana. There are also some excellent hybrid weigelas, four of the best being the pink Abel Carriére, Bouquet Rose, the flesh-pink Heroine, and the deep **crimson** Eva Rathke.

Left *Rosa floribunda Plentiful has fully double flowers of warm pink. "Roses" wrote Robert Herrick "at first were white". True or not, they are now in almost every gradation of colour from white to darkest crimson*
Opposite *Floribunda roses, especially, have been vastly improved and developed in recent years. Several different kinds are shown on these two pages. As well as the popular Iceberg and Plentiful, the golden Allgold, pink Arakan scarlet Lilli Marlene are all great new Floribunda roses*

Above *Rosa damascena variegata – the old York and Lancaster rose, has petals that are parti-coloured in white and pink*

Above left *Rosa moschata Felicia is one of the most sweetly scented of the Musk roses*

Left *Flowers to "bid the rash gazer wipe his eye" are borne by floribunda roses, such as Rosemary or Frensham*

Opposite above *White floribunda rose Iceberg, one of the most popular of all modern roses*

Below *A corner of the famous rose garden at Haddon Hall*

Right *Floribunda roses such as pink Oberon and white Iceberg in a border planted with santolina and shrubby Salvia officinalis atropurpurea, the Purple Sage*

Index

Page numbers in italics refer to coloured illustrations

Index of People and Places